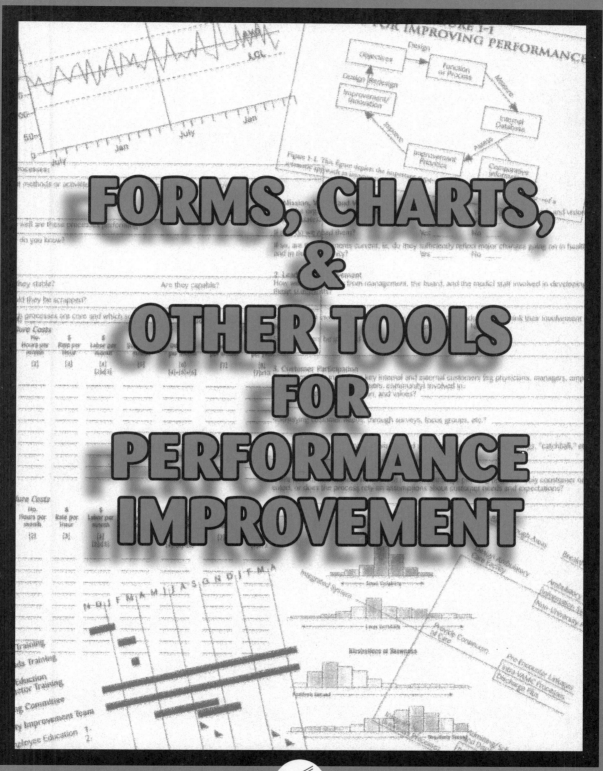

FORMS, CHARTS, & OTHER TOOLS FOR PERFORMANCE IMPROVEMENT

Joint Commission Mission

The mission of the Joint Commission on Accreditation of Healthcare Organizations is to improve the quality of care provided to the public.

SECTIONS:

C
O
N
T
E
N
T
S

6: DATA COLLECTION TOOLS

7: DATA-DISPLAY TOOLS

8: CAUSAL-ANALYSIS TOOLS

9: TOOLS FOR SELECTING AND IMPLEMENTING IMPROVEMENTS

10: TOOLS FOR KEEPING TEAMS ON TRACK AND KEEPING TRACK OF TEAMS

OVERVIEW

OVERVIEW

This book presents a compilation of forms, charts, and other useful tools for implementing key factors of desirable performance through effective performance improvement efforts. These factors of desirable performance include

- leadership commitment;
- attention to organizational vision, mission, and values;
- employee empowerment;
- systems thinking;
- focus on functions and processes;
- attention to customer-supplier relationships;
- attention to customer and supplier needs and expectations;
- teamwork;
- careful planning and design of new processes, including the improvement process;
- valid and reliable performance measurement;
- insightful assessment of performance data;
- carefully planned, tested, and implemented improvement actions; and
- sharing successes throughout the organization.

Experience has shown health care professionals that these factors cannot be put into action simply by acknowledging their importance. People need a means to enact them. Therefore, health care professionals have searched for specific methods, tools, and techniques to incorporate these factors into the daily work of their organizations.

The result has been a bevy of improvement methods, tools, and techniques that seek to systematize and synthesize these and other principles to improve performance. For example, techniques such as Hoshin planning and force-field analysis have helped organizations in strategic planning endeavors; methods such as Hospital Corporation of America's FOCUS-PDCA and the Joint Commission's ten-step process have helped establish processes for improvement; techniques such as multivoting have helped groups set priorities and reach consensus; tools such as flowcharts have helped illustrate organizations' processes; tools such as run charts and control charts have allowed organizations to assess performance data; and methods such as critical paths have helped design or redesign a process.

Your colleagues have developed the forms, charts, and tools in this book for use in their performance improvement efforts. Some of the tools in this book, such as flowcharts and run charts, are widely recognized; some others are home-grown forms, questionnaires, data-collection tools, and storyboards, tailored to a specific organization's needs. Some reflect a departmental focus rather than the functional focus that Joint Commission standards are being revised to reflect. In general, this book presents tools that lend themselves to concise explanations and practical, specific outputs. The Joint Commission's book *Using Quality Improvement Tools in a Health Care Setting* offers more detailed explanations of how select tools are used. And the book *Process Improvement Models: Case Studies in Health Care* describes several performance-improvement methods, within which these tools can be used.

This book represents the collective knowledge of health care professionals, allowing readers to benefit from the experience of countless colleagues. By collecting many performance improvement tools currently used in the health care field, the Joint Commission hopes to give readers a chance to review their colleagues' improvement tools and to consider their use or adaptation. To that end, this book is inclusive rather than exclusive; this collection gathers an array of tools from many different organizations and settings. These tools reflect different improvement methods and philosophies. All will not be amenable to all organizations.

Since your colleagues have so generously shared this information, we hope you will do the same. If you have a form, chart, or tool that you find particularly useful in your performance improvement activities, the Joint Commission's publications department would like to hear from you. Your tool could potentially be published in a subsequent edition of this book. Please send in a copy of the tool to: Joint Commission on Accreditation of Healthcare Organizations, Department of Publications, General Publications, One Renaissance Boulevard, Oakbrook Terrace, IL 60181.

How to Use this Book

The tools in this book are organized in practical categories that represent each tool's basic type and function:

- *Organizational planning and assessment tools.* These tools can help an organization analyze its overall strengths and weaknesses, choose areas on which to focus improvement efforts, assess its readiness for performance improvement, and assess the effectiveness of performance improvement efforts.
- *Customer analysis and survey tools.* These tools can help an organization identify its key customers and gather performance-related information from those customers (especially patients).
- *Flowcharts.* Flowcharts help document current processes, redesign current processes, and design new processes. This section shows several different types of flowcharts.
- *Critical paths and practice guidelines.* Critical paths document basic treatment procedures for certain diagnoses in an effort to eliminate unnecessary variation. This section presents various forms and uses of this tool.
- *Data collection tools.* This section includes a tool for planning data collection, in addition to tools for indicator data collection, patient/client health status assessment, and adverse drug reaction reports.
- *Data display tools.* This section includes run charts, control charts, and other methods to illustrate performance and help detect trends and patterns.
- *Causal analysis tools.* These tools, which include cause-and-effect diagrams and Pareto charts, help determine the underlying causes of performance problems or conditions and, thus, potential areas for improvement.
- *Tools for selecting and implementing improvements.* These tools can help teams select improvement actions, test those actions, and implement the actions in a systematic way.
- *Tools for keeping teams on track and keeping track of teams.* This section contains a variety of tools to document team activities and to guide teams through the steps necessary to measure, assess, and improve processes.

The tools collected in this publication can be used or adapted for many different performance improvement activities. For example, a flowchart can be used to design a new process or to assess an existing process, and a Gantt chart can be used to establish a timetable for implementing sweeping change in an organization (for example, continuous quality improvement) or for testing a relatively limited change (for example, a new staffing procedure in a single unit).

Most of the tools in this book can be used in the Joint Commission's *cycle for improving performance.* This cycle identifies the important steps involved in systematic improvement:

- design;
- measure;
- assess; and
- improve.

Many of the tools can be used in more than one step in the cycle.

A brief explanation of each step follows. This explanation should give readers a sense of how the tools can help with a systematic, organizationwide approach to improvement. Figure 1-1, page 9, illustrates the cycle.

The Joint Commission's Cycle for Improving Performance

Design

As health care organizations attempt to better serve their patients and communities, and compete more effectively, many are designing and offering new services or redesigning their services to be more efficient, to be attentive to customer expectations, and to improve patient outcomes.

As illustrated in Figure 1-1, below, the inputs for design are *objectives*; organization leaders must decide what they want the new design to accomplish. The outputs from design are *functions and processes*. Rather than focusing on individual tasks as the means to fulfill organizational objectives, effective design efforts consider how many tasks are coordinated into functions and processes that can effectively and efficiently achieve objectives.

Systematic planning and implementation are key to the design of any function or process and should include

- reviewing organizational goals and the activities that fulfill them;
- reviewing and selecting new opportunities that require a new design effort;
- designing the new function or process; and
- measuring and assessing the performance of the new process or function.

Such a systematic process helps an organization confirm that it

- can identify opportunities for innovation;
- fairly and fully weighs the benefits and drawbacks of a newly designed process or function;
- involves the right people and gets the best knowledge for creating the design; and
- can determine whether the results of the design effort meet the objectives.

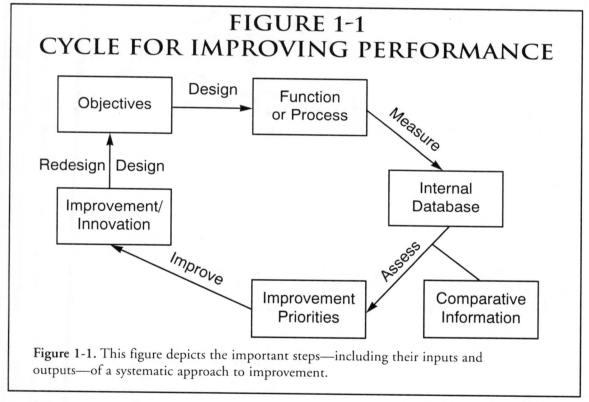

FIGURE 1-1
CYCLE FOR IMPROVING PERFORMANCE

Figure 1-1. This figure depicts the important steps—including their inputs and outputs—of a systematic approach to improvement.

When planning for and designing new functions and processes, the following should be fully considered:

- The organization's mission (its overriding purpose), vision (how it sees itself in the future), and strategic plan (strategies for carrying out its mission and fulfilling its vision).
- Needs and expectations of patients, staff, and other important groups such as accreditors and payers. These people make up the vital customers and suppliers for any process. One goal of any process design should be to meet customer and supplier needs and fulfill expectations.
- Current knowledge about organizational and clinical activities. Any new process needs to consider current activities within the organization, as well as best practices outside the organization.
- Relevant data. Successfully designed processes are based on data. For example, any new information management system must consider data about the current information needs of the organization.

- Availability of resources. Given the limited resources in health care today, the benefits of any new process should be weighed against the necessary funds, staff time, equipment, and so forth.
- Customer-supplier relationships. Any newly designed process should facilitate the greatest efficiency in these relationships. It is also important to recognize that many of the internal customer-supplier "hand offs" in a process take place across departmental lines.

Measure

To improve a process, an organization needs valid, reliable data. The goal of measurement is to collect that data. In today's environment, measurement is an especially pressing concern for all health care professionals. The need to demonstrate effectiveness and efficiency requires organizations to quantify their performance with measures of patient health outcomes and resource use.

For many years the Joint Commission has been engaged in performance measurement through its standards and surveys. Currently, the Joint Commission is expanding its measurement capabilities by implementing its Indicator Measurement System (IMSystem), which involves continuous collection of performance information related to specific indicators. The information will be used by health care organizations to improve performance, by the Joint Commission to evaluate health care organizations' performance, and by other interested users—such as purchasers and payers—to make decisions about health care. The IMSystem is being introduced in stages to organizations seeking accreditation. At first, participation will be voluntary, and the system will comprise 25 indicators focusing on obstetrical and perioperative care. Each year, more indicators will be introduced until a full complement of performance measures is in place. At that time, participation in the IMSystem will become an integral component of the accreditation process.

Measurement and performance improvement.
Measurement is important at several stages in the improvement process. Measurement provides data about current performance. For some processes, such measurement should be continuous and result in a database about performance over time. For other processes, it is only necessary to measure to provide a baseline when an organization has decided to examine that process for possible improvement opportunities.

Once an organization decides to improve a process, it needs to measure performance. Even if the process has been continuously measured, an improvement effort may need more detailed data in order to understand the process and take the necessary improvement actions.

Measurement continues to be important once an improvement action has been tested, and after it has been fully implemented, to determine whether improvement has occurred and the degree of that improvement.

The subjects of measurement.
The decision about which processes to measure—either continuously or as part of a specific improvement effort—should be based on various criteria. The Joint Commission standards offer criteria for selecting those processes. For example, the *1995 Accreditation Manual for Hospitals* (*AMH*) asks that organizations collect data about

- processes related to the important functions identified in the manual (for example, assessment of patients, care of patients, leadership, among others);
- high-volume, high-risk, and/or problem-prone processes; and
- processes related to use of operative and other invasive procedures, use of medications, use of blood and blood components, and determination of the appropriateness of admissions and continued hospitalization.

According to the *1995 AMH*, data collected should address processes and outcomes and pertain to needs and expectations of patients and others. Organization leaders should consider many other factors when deciding what to measure, including the organization's

- mission;
- vision;
- resources; and
- provider, patient, community, purchaser, and payer concerns.

Types of measurement. Measurement is based on indicators that articulate the specific information to be collected. An indicator is a *valid and reliable quantitative process or outcome measure related to one or more dimensions of performance.* The dimensions of performance include efficacy, appropriateness, availability, timeliness, effectiveness, continuity, safety, efficacy, and respect and caring.

Two important types of indicators are *sentinel-event* indicators and *aggregate-data* indicators. A sentinel-event indicator identifies an individual event or phenomenon that is significant enough to trigger further review each time it occurs. Maternal death is an example of a sentinel-event indicator. Most sentinel events are undesirable and occur infrequently. In contrast, an aggregate-data indicator quantifies a process or outcome related to many cases. Unlike sentinel events, an event identified by an aggregate-data indicator may occur frequently and may be desirable or undesirable. Two examples of aggregate data indicators are

- number of reported medication errors; and
- patients delivered by cesarean section.

Assess

Assessment means translating data collected during measurement into information that can be used to change processes and improve performance. This assessment takes a number of different forms. Health care professionals assess data about current performance to identify any need for improvement; they assess processes to understand how they are carried out; they assess the causes of current performance to help target actions for improvement; and they assess data about how a process performs after an improvement action has been taken.

As illustrated in Figure 1-1, assessment uses comparative information to set improvement priorities. Most assessment requires comparing data to a reference point. Reference points include

- historical patterns of performance in the organization;
- performance in many other organizations as represented in aggregate external reference databases;
- practice guidelines and other scientific sources;
- desired performance control limits, standards, specifications, and targets; and
- external benchmarks or best practices.

Historical patterns of performance in the organization. When an organization has accumulated a sufficient fund of data, it is able to compare current performance to historical patterns. This comparison can take many forms. For example, an organization may compare current performance with levels during the previous year, and it may compare performance levels for various days of the week, various shifts, or various parts of the organization.

Aggregate external reference databases. In addition to comparing performance within their organization, organizations can compare their performance with other organizations. This wider scope of comparison can help an organization draw conclusions about its own performance. Comparison with aggregate external databases takes various forms. One example of an external database is the Joint Commission's IMSystem. Aggregate, risk-adjusted data about specific indicators can help an organization's leaders decide how to set priorities for improvement by showing whether its current performance is inside or outside the expected range. Health care systems often have systemwide databases that feed information about certain indicators (for example, outcomes, costs, and lengths of stay for certain treatments) back to member organizations for use in their individual performance-improvement activities. Payers also aggregate information about performance and cost, as do governments at the state and federal level.

Practice guidelines/parameters. Practice guidelines/parameters, critical paths, and other scientifically based descriptions of patient care processes and procedures are useful reference points for comparison. Whether these procedures are developed by professional societies, expert panels, or in-house practitioners, they represent an expert consensus about the best practices for a given diagnosis, treatment, or procedure. Assessing variation from such established procedures can help an organization identify opportunities for improvement.

Desired performance limits. Organizations may also establish control limits, specifications, or targets against which to compare current performance. Control limits are statistically derived limits to show whether a process is stable. Unstable processes must be brought within control limits before any lasting improvement efforts can be made. Performance specifications and targets are not derived from statistics, but are based on what the process must accomplish and on the expectations of customers.

Benchmarking. Another method of comparing performance is benchmarking. Like using an external reference database, benchmarking involves comparing one organization's performance with performance outside that organization. Benchmarking is predicated on in-depth study of how other organizations routinely perform key processes and consistently achieve good outcomes.

Certain kinds of assessment also require learning what factors cause current performance. This knowledge is gained by studying a process; identifying its steps and decision points; identifying the various people, actions, and equipment required for the process' outcome; finding links between variables in performance; and ranking the frequency of causes. Tools such as flowcharts, cause-and-effect diagrams, and Pareto charts—all found in this book—are useful in studying a process and identifying potential areas for improvement.

Intensive assessment of a process should result in identifying root causes for its performance, and should set priorities among those causes. Because a significant investment of time and effort is usually needed to implement improvement, organizations must consider their mission, strategic plans, resources, and other such issues when setting improvement priorities.

Improve

With the knowledge gained through measurement and assessment, it is possible to take effective action to improve processes. Such action often involves refining or redesigning a process to improve its level of performance.

Health care organizations have found that a uniform, yet flexible, improvement method helps ensure that improvement actions *address root causes, involve the right people,* and *result in desired and sustained changes.* One well-established process for improvement is the plan-do-study-act (PDSA) cycle (also called the plan-do-check-act [PDCA] cycle). This process is ascribed to Walter Shewhart, a quality pioneer with Bell Laboratories in the 1920s and 1930s. The process is also widely associated with W. Edwards Deming, a follower of Shewhart. Deming made PDSA central to his influential teachings about quality. The cycle is compelling in its logic, simplicity, and continuous nature. A brief explanation of this process should help clarify the essential activities involved in taking improvement actions.

Plan. Plan, in this context, means to gather the data and other information to be used in developing a tentative improvement action and then to create an operational plan for testing the chosen improvement action. Small-scale testing is necessary to determine whether an improvement action is viable, whether it will have the desired result, and whether any refinements are necessary before putting the action into full operation. Planning involves determining who will be involved in the test, what they need to know to participate in the test, the testing timetables, how the test will be implemented, why the idea is being tested, what the success factors are, and how the process and outcomes of the test will be measured and assessed. The list of proposed improvement actions should be narrowed to a number that can be reasonably tested—perhaps between two and four, not often more.

Do. Do means to implement the pilot test and collect actual performance data.

Study. Study involves analyzing the data collected during the pilot test. This analysis seeks to learn whether the improvement action was wholly successful, partly successful, or not successful in achieving the desired outcome(s). To determine degree of success, compare actual test performance to desired performance targets and to baseline results achieved using the usual process.

Act. The next step of the process is act. If the actions tested are not successful, the cycle repeats by testing a different improvement idea or testing the previous improvement idea with modifications or in different circumstances. Once actions are proven successful, they are made part of everyday operating procedure. The process does not stop here. The effectiveness of the action continues to be assessed. In addition, the cycle as a whole repeats: an organization continues to plan, do, study, and act to improve its many processes and services.

Whether organizations follow this exact process or not, its components should be part of improvement efforts.

Using the Cycle for Improving Performance

Once an organization has completed a turn through this cycle for a given function or process, the cycle continues. The objectives are reviewed and perhaps changed. Measurement continues in order to determine whether improvement has occurred and is sustained. The internal database continues to grow. And assessment using the ever-growing information base may identify further opportunities for improvement.

This cycle is anchored in the real work of an organization—the functions and processes it carries out every day to pursue goals narrow and broad. This cycle can be carried out by natural workgroups as part of everyday activities. When the process or function being addressed crosses unit or departmental boundaries, however, it may be necessary to identify or form a specific team composed of the people who are responsible for the process, who carry out the process, and who are affected by the process. For more information on the Joint Commission's cycle for improving performance read *Framework for Improving Performance: From Principles to Practice.*

The Joint Commission's Standards

The *1995 AMH* contains a chapter called "Improving Organizational Performance." These standards can also be found in the *1995 Accreditation Manual for Home Care* and the *1995 Accreditation Manual for Mental Health, Chemical Dependency, and Mental Retardation/Developmental Disabilities Services.* By 1996 all Joint Commission standards manuals will have "Improving Organizational Performance" standards. Although the standards in this chapter require that organizations improve their performance in a planned and systematic manner, the standards do not prescribe the specific approach or the specific tools to be used, including those described in this book. These tools can, however, help organizations develop an individualized approach to meeting the standards, one consistent with the organization's size, patient population, mission, and culture.

For example, standard PI.4 articulates this performance expectation:

The organization has a systematic process to assess collected data in order to determine
- whether design specifications for new processes were met;
- the level of performance and stability of important existing processes;
- priorities for possible improvement of existing processes;
- actions to improve the performance of processes; and
- whether changes in the processes resulted in improvement.

This expectation focuses on the goals of assessment rather than how that assessment is carried out. In fact, the Joint Commission standards are written to encourage creative approaches to fulfilling the performance expectations.

That is how this book can help. The tools presented here can be seen as a menu of different approaches to improving performance and fulfilling the standards' specific performance expectations. To continue the example above (standard PI.4), this book offers several specific approaches to assessing data that organizations can use to fulfill this standard and—more important—to gain the information necessary to improve organizational performance.

The cycle for improving performance described on pages 8–13 corresponds to the structure of the "Improving Organizational Performance" standards. (Figure 1-2, below, illustrates the pertinent standards.) Keep in mind, however, that the contents of this book do not pertain solely to the "Improving Organizational Performance" standards. This book presents tools and techniques that will help improve performance in all the organization's important functions, including

- assessment of patients;
- care of patients;
- education of patients and family;
- continuum of care;
- leadership;
- management of information;
- management of human resources;
- management of the environment of care; and
- surveillance, prevention, and control of infection.

The goal, of course, should not simply be to fulfill Joint Commission standards. It is hoped that this book will help organizations pursue the excellence in patient care that is the core of their mission.

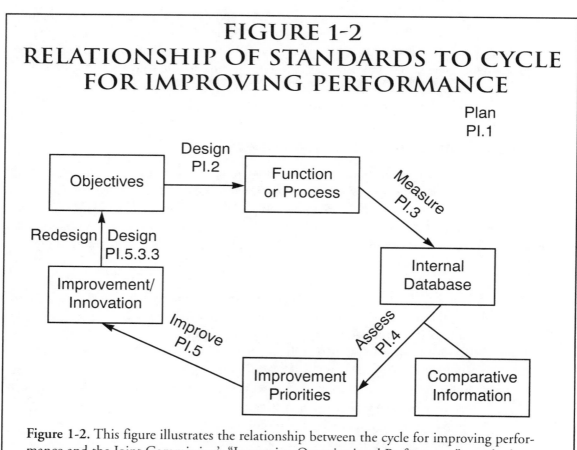

FIGURE 1-2
RELATIONSHIP OF STANDARDS TO CYCLE FOR IMPROVING PERFORMANCE

Figure 1-2. This figure illustrates the relationship between the cycle for improving performance and the Joint Commission's "Improving Organizational Performance" standards from the *1995 Accreditation Manual for Hospitals.*

ORGANIZATIONAL PLANNING AND ASSESSMENT TOOLS

These tools can help an organization analyze its overall strengths and weaknesses, choose areas on which to focus improvement efforts, assess its readiness for performance improvement, and assess the effectiveness of its performance-improvement efforts.

SECTION TWO

FIGURE 2-1
FORCE-FIELD ANALYSIS, PART A

Below, list all the factors in your organization that will lead toward a positive resolution. Next, list all the negative factors that may impede resolution. The factors identified may be people, policies, organizational structure, or cultural issues, for example.

Driving Forces

Restraining Forces

Figure 2-1. This two-part figure illustrates a planning tool called "force-field analysis," a method by which an organization (or team) can identify and enhance the forces that lead it toward its goals—"driving forces"—and can identify and minimize those that prevent attaining those goals—"restraining forces."

FIGURE 2-1
FORCE-FIELD ANALYSIS, PART B

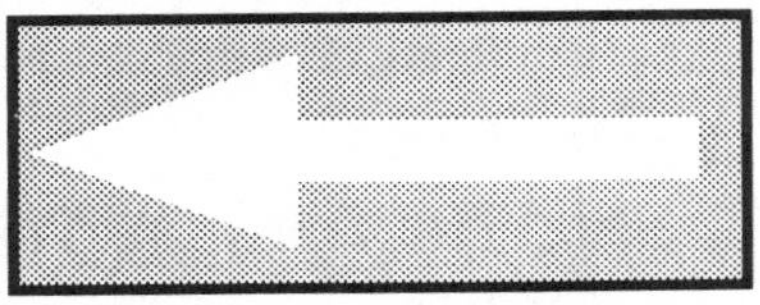

Strategies to
Enhance
Driving Forces

_____

_____

_____

_____

_____

_____

_____

Strategies to
Minimize
Restraining Forces

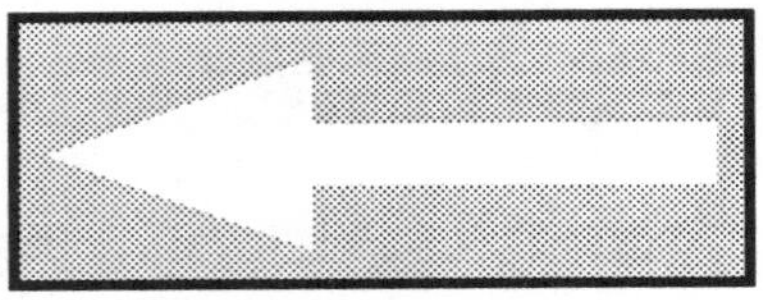

_____

_____

_____

_____

_____

_____

_____

FIGURE 2-2
HOSHIN PLANNING

	Breakthrough Areas	**Breakthrough Projects**
	Design Ambulatory Care System	Ambulatory Care Facility
		Information System
		Non-University Practitioners
HOSHIN		
	Provide Continuum of Care	Pre-Encounter Linkages
Integrated Systems		Intra-VAMC* Processes
		Discharge Plus
	Integrate Key Business Processes	Admitting/Scheduling and Discharge
		Billing/Collecting
		External Relations
		Finance/Marketing

*VAMC = Vermont Academic Medical Center

Figure 2-2. Hoshin is a Japanese term that describes a step-by-step process for building consensus on the vital few strategic areas in which breakthroughs must occur if an organization is to meet and exceed the needs of its customers. The focus is generally on customer satisfaction and fundamental process improvement. This tree diagram illustrates the breakthrough areas and projects that must be developed or improved for the medical center's hoshin to be achieved.

Source: Demers DM: Tutorial: Implementing hoshin planning at the Vermont Academic Medical Center. *Quality Management in Health Care* 1(4): 69, 1993. Used with permission of David M. Demers, MPH, Medical Center Hospital of Vermont, Burlington, Vermont, 1993.

FIGURE 2-3
ORGANIZATION ANALYSIS WORKSHEET

1. Products and/or Services:

What are the products and/or services that you produce?

2. Customers:

Who are your customers? Who uses your products and/or services?
(This could include internal as well as external customers.)

Figure 2-3. This worksheet helps an organization view itself as a system, begin a system analysis, and decide on processes to improve. The worksheet can be completed organizationwide or departmentwide.

Source: Developed in a collaborative effort between Executive Learning, Inc and the Quality Resources Group at Hospital Corporation of America. Used with permission.

FIGURE 2-3 (CONTINUED)
ORGANIZATION ANALYSIS WORKSHEET

3. Needs that Products/Services Meet:

What is the underlying social, community, or organizational need that your customers have for your products and/or services?

Do your products and/or services represent the best way to meet these needs?

What might do the job better?

4. Customer Knowledge:

What measures do your customers use when they judge the quality of what you produce?

What prompts customers to use these measures?

Why do your competitor's customers not use your products and/or services?

FIGURE 2-3 (CONTINUED)
ORGANIZATION ANALYSIS WORKSHEET

5. Processes:

What methods or activitites do you use to make your products and/or services?

How well are these processes performing?

How do you know?

Are they stable?   Are they capable?

Should they be scrapped?

Which processes are core and which support core processes?

6. Inputs:

What comes into your processes and is changed by the process to create the services or products?

How good are the products and/or services you receive?

How do you know?

What could you measure?

FIGURE 2-3 (CONTINUED)
ORGANIZATION ANALYSIS WORKSHEET

7. Suppliers:

What departments, organizations, or people provide the inputs to your processes?

How are they working to improve the products and/or services they provide?

What is your relationship with them?

8. Vision:

Based on your knowledge of your customers and of the underlying social need your organization meets, what is the aim for the future in your organization?

FIGURE 2-3 (CONTINUED)
ORGANIZATION ANALYSIS WORKSHEET

9. Strategic Initiatives:

Based on your vision (and vision of the organization), knowledge of the customer, and information from those knowledgeable about your processes, what are three or four areas/objectives that are strategically important to improve now?

10. Incrementally Improve:

Improvement of which specific processes will create the greatest movement toward the strategic improvements sought by the organization?

How do you know there is a relationship between these processes and the strategic initiatives?

Don't forget to consider processes within your suppliers' organizations as well. What other processes affect the processes you have selected for improvement?

FIGURE 2-4
PROFILE OF A QUALITY-TROUBLED COMPANY

Characteristic

	That's us all the way	Some is true	We're not like that
1. Our services and/or products normally contain waivers, deviations, and other indications of their not conforming to requirements.			
2. We have a "fix it" oriented field service and/or dealer organization.			
3. Our employees do not know what management wants from them concerning quality.			
4. Management does not know what the price of performance really is.			
5. Management believes that quality is a problem caused by something other than management action.			

Point Count Condition

21–25	Critical:	Needs intensive care immediately.
16–20	Guarded:	Needs life support system hookup.
11–15	Resting:	Needs medication and attention.
6–10	Healing:	Needs regular checkup.
5	Whole:	Needs counseling.

Figure 2-4. This figure, designed by Philip Crosby, can be used by organization leaders to determine the need for a revamped approach to quality improvement.

Source: Reprinted with permission from Crosby PB: *Quality Without Tears.* New York: McGraw-Hill Book Company, 1984, p 4.

FIGURE 2-5
DEPARTMENTAL MATRIX

Departmental Matrix			Department: _____		
Indicators	Impact	Process 1	Process 2	Process 3	Key Quality Characteristic
PHYSICIAN					
Available Time					
Scheduling					
Nurses					
Timely Reports					
Accessible Consultation					
Equipment					
Employee QI					
Treated as Customers					

Indicators	Impact	Process 1	Process 2	Process 3	Key Quality Characteristic
PATIENT					
Clinical Outcome					
Response TLC					
Nurses					
Living Arrangements					
Billing and Collections					
Admission					
Discharge					

Figure 2-5. This matrix is used to identify key processes for a department. These key processes can then be considered for future improvement efforts. The left column of the matrix contains key indicators of high quality as determined by four customer groups: physicians, patients, employees, and payers. In the next column, labeled "impact," the department identifies the degree of influence it has on each indicator. The next three columns allow the department to identify the processes it performs that relate to the specific indicator. In the last column, the department identifies the "key quality characteristic" (such as timeliness, accessibility, and so forth) associated with the indicator. Figure 2-6 (page 28) illustrates a partially completed matrix.

Source: West Paces Medical Center, Atlanta, GA. Used with permission.

FIGURE 2-5 (CONTINUED)
DEPARTMENTAL MATRIX

EMPLOYEE	Impact	Process 1	Process 2	Process 3	Key Quality Characteristic
Nurses					
Departments Work Together					
Top Leaders Understand					
Image					
Qualified Co-workers					
Efficient Processes					

PAYERS					
Employees Brag					
Costs Less than Competitors					
Reduce Costs and Improve Quality					

Instructions: Review list of hospital quality indicators listed by customer group (physician, patient, employee, and payer). Indicate the degree of impact your department has on each quality indicator by entering the appropriate symbol in the impact column. List tree processes that directly relate to the outcome of customer satisfaction for each indicator. Choose a total of three processes that relate to a "heavy" impact indicator from which the QIC will select one as your first opportunity for improvement.

● = Heavy   ■ = Moderate   ▲ = Slight   ---- = None

FIGURE 2-6
SAMPLE DEPARTMENTAL MATRIX

Department: 3 West		● = Heavy	■ = Moderate	▲ = Slight
Indicators	**Impact**	**Process 1**	**Process 2**	**Process 3**
Available Time	●	MD rounds update	Chart procedure	Procedure assist.
Scheduling	▲	Requis. process		
Nurses	●	MD rounds update	Chart procedure	Complic. notif.
Timely Reports	■	Filing	Ab. result notif.	Requis. process
Accessible Consultation	▲	Order notif.		
Equipment				
Clinical Outcome	●	Acute MI	Bronchitis	Heart failure
Response TLC	●	Pain medication	Nourishment	Call-light response
Nurses	●	Patient condition inform.	RN skills assmt/CE	Complaint notification
Living Arrangements	■	Complaint notification	DC cleaning	Diet order
Admission	▲	DC cleaning		
Discharge	●	DC notification	DC instructions	Transport

MD=physician; MI=myocardial infarction; RN=registered nurse; DC=discharge

Figure 2-6. This figure shows how the departmental matrix in Figure 2-5 could be completed for one customer group (physicians).

Source: West Paces Medical Center, Atlanta, GA. Used with permission.

FIGURE 2-7
IMPLEMENTATION PLAN FOR TOTAL QUALITY MANAGEMENT

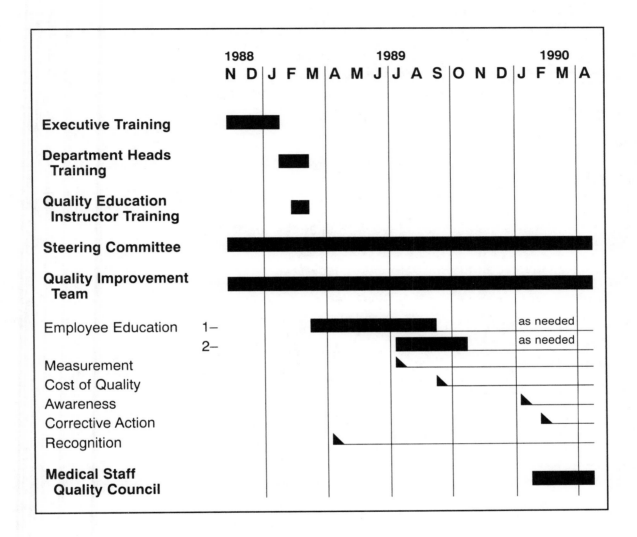

Figure 2-7. This figure displays how Winter Park Memorial Hospital (Winter Park, FL) illustrated its implementation plan for quality management.

Source: Hughes JM: Total quality management in a 300-bed community hospital: The quality improvement process translated to health care. *QRB,* Sep 1992, p 294. © 1992 Joint Commission on Accreditation of Healthcare Organizations.

FIGURE 2-8
PLANNING/QUALITY ASSESSMENT TOOL

1. Mission, Vision, and Values

Does the organization have statements of mission (purpose), values (guiding beliefs), and vision (future state)? Yes_____ No _____

If not, do we need them? Yes_____ No _____

If so, are the statements current, that is, do they sufficiently reflect major changes going on in health care and in the community? Yes_____ No _____

2. Leadership Involvement

How were key leaders from management, the board, and the medical staff involved in developing these statements? _____

_____

Is this level of involvement sufficient? Have we asked the leaders if they think their involvement is sufficient? Yes_____ No _____

Should leaders be involved more or differently? How? _____

_____

3. Customer Participation

To what extent is input from key internal and external customers (for example, physicians, managers, employees, patients, families, purchasers, community) involved in:

• Developing the mission, vision, and values? _____

_____

• Identifying customer needs through surveys, focus groups, and so on? _____

_____

• Refining initial drafts of mission, vision, and strategic initiatives through meetings, "catchball," and so on? _____

_____

Is this level of involvement sufficient to make the strategic planning process truly customer oriented, or does the process rely on assumptions about customer needs and expectations? _____

_____

Figure 2-8. Senior management can use this tool to assess how well their organization's planning process reflects total quality principles.

Source: How well does your organization's strategic planning process reflect total quality philosophies? A management assessment and planning tool. *The Quality Letter for Healthcare Leaders,* pp 25–27, Sep 1993, published by Bader & Associates, Inc. Used with permission.

FIGURE 2-8 (CONTINUED)
PLANNING/QUALITY ASSESSMENT TOOL

4. Communication and Alignment with Daily Work Life

After the mission, values, vision, and strategic initiatives are adopted, to what extent are they communicated to key persons throughout the organization?_____

_____

Can managers and employees articulate how their jobs reflect the organization's mission and vision?   Yes_____   No _____

Are current efforts to communicate the mission and vision and to integrate them with daily work life sufficient? How can they be improved? _____

_____

5. Culture and Empowerment

To what extent does the organizational culture support employee involvement in the strategic planning process? Do employees believe the organization is committed to empowerment? _____

_____

Are these efforts sufficient? How can they be improved? _____

_____

6. Alignment of Strategic Goals and Quality Planning

How is the strategic planning process used to identify opportunities for improvement throughout the organization? _____

_____

Conversely, how is information from quality management activities used to establish strategic priorities? _____

_____

Do strategic planning and TQM generate customer-oriented performance measures that are used as management and improvement tools throughout the organization? _____

_____

Are the above activities sufficient? How could they be improved? _____

_____

7. Systems Thinking

Does the strategic planning process view the organization as a system, looking at the interrelationships among departments and key processes as they relate to customers?
                    Yes_____   No _____

How could the strategic planning and CQI processes enhance their use of systems thinking? _____

FIGURE 2-9
TOTAL QUALITY MANAGEMENT ASSESSMENT

	5	4	3	2	1	0
LEADERSHIP						
1. Senior management is personally involved in quality-related activities such as planning, assessment, and review of quality plans and progress, quality teams, giving and receiving quality training, and recognition of employees.						
2. There is a quality vision, quality policy, guidelines, and other documented statements of quality values. These have been communicated throughout the organization and are accepted by all employees.						
3. We have clearly defined customer satisfaction and quality improvement objectives. Roles, responsibilities, and involvement at all levels of management in quality improvement are understood and accepted. We allocate adequate resources to quality improvement and awareness.						
INFORMATION AND ANALYSIS						
4. We have quality information systems that we routinely use in managing, evaluating, and planning for quality. These systems include data on customers, suppliers, internal operations, patient health status outcomes, quality measurements of the services we provide, and competitive comparisons.						
5. We routinely analyze these data to identify opportunities or problems, to determine the root causes of problems, to design countermeasures or remedies to address the root causes, and to ascertain whether our countermeasures or remedies have produced the expected results.						
STRATEGIC PLANNING						
6. We have specific quality goals and objectives in our business plans and strategic plans. These include the integration of continuous improvement activities of all work units into plans and employees' involvement in planning.						
MANAGEMENT						
7. All employees have the opportunity to participate in quality improvement. They have wide authority to act individually. They have the right and obligation to act in any case of potential quality deficiencies or compromises.						
8. Quality improvement teams are active at all levels of the organization. Employees participate within functional units, in cross-functional teams, and with suppliers and other external groups as appropriate. Physicians take an active role.						
9. Quality training and education are widespread. All new employees receive quality orientation. Training in statistical and other quantitative methods is available to appropriate categories of employees. The effectiveness of quality education is routinely evaluated and the training is continuously improved.						

Figure 2-9. This tool can be used to assess an organization's quality-improvement initiative—in particular, leadership performance. The tool is completed by department heads and senior managers.

Source: Assessing the progress of the TQM initiative: A leadership assessment tool. *The Quality Letter for Healthcare Leaders,* pp 22-23, Jul-Aug 1992, published by Bader & Associates, Inc Used with permission.

FIGURE 2-9 (CONTINUED)
TOTAL QUALITY MANAGEMENT ASSESSMENT

	5	4	3	2	1	0
QUALITY ASSURANCE OF PRODUCTS AND SERVICES						
10. There is a working process for determining and converting customer needs and expectations to product, process, and service specifications. We have a detailed central plan that includes how we select key process characteristics to be controlled and describes how they are to be controlled.						
11. We routinely verify that our quality requirements are being met by suppliers and all external providers of goods and services, including those with whom we coordinate patient care.						
QUALITY RESULTS						
12. We have clear measures of services quality based on customer needs and expectations. We have documented evidence of continuous improvement in all key areas.						
13. We routinely make comparisons of health status outcomes or service quality levels through independent reports, analyses, and our own evaluations. We are among the best in our key service areas based on our comparisons with national industry leaders.						
14. We have clear measures of health status outcomes among our patients and we have documented evidence of continuous improvement in clinical outcomes and patient well-being.						
CUSTOMER SATISFACTION						
15. We have a clear and working process for identifying the needs and expectations of patient constituencies and potential patients. We routinely measure how well we are meeting these needs.						
16. We have a clear and working process for identifying the needs and expectations of physician constituencies. We routinely measure how well we are meeting these needs.						
17. We make it easy for customers to share concerns. We actively solicit complaints and customer feedback. Complaints made to different parts of the organization are centrally reviewed and analyzed. We analyze the complaints to determine root causes and use our analyses to drive prevention efforts and continuous improvement.						
18. We frequently measure the key areas of customer satisfaction. Our trends in customer satisfaction indicators provide evidence of continuous improvement and our position among the leaders in our industry nationwide.						

Comments:
What would help you better achieve your quality responsibilities and goals? Please be specific in terms of training, policies, information systems, corporate support, and so forth.

For each question, rate your perception of the organization's performance using the following 0 to 5 scale:
0—I DO NOT KNOW the answer
1—Does NOT DESCRIBE any activities
2—Describes or applies to SOME activities in SOME departments
3—Describes or applies to MANY activities in MANY departments
4—Describes or applies to MOST activities in MOST departments
5—Describes or applies to ALL activities in ALL departments

FIGURE 2-10
MISSION EFFECTIVENESS OPINIONNAIRE

Directions: Please circle the number after each statement which best reflects your experience of the statement as it applies to your facility. If you are unable to make a choice, please circle the "?" in the "Don't Know" column.

	Low	Moderate	High	Don't Know
1. As an employee of this facility you are aware that it is a Catholic institution.	1	2	3	?
2. As an employee of this facility you are aware of and received information concerning its philosophy and value system.	1	2	3	?
3. As an employee of this facility you are made aware of its mission statement.	1	2	3	?
4. In general you are aware of the sponsorship of this facility by the Congregation of Alexian Brothers and the "Alexian Spirit" they foster.	1	2	3	?
5. This facility displays various symbols which reflect its religious tradition.	1	2	3	?

Comments on 1–5: _____

_____

	Low	Moderate	High	Don't Know
6. Employees are treated with respect by their supervisors/managers.	1	2	3	?
7. Support from co-workers is readily experienced within your department.	1	2	3	?
8. Employees are encouraged by their supervisors to develop and use their skills and talents.	1	2	3	?
9. This facility offers a just salary and benefit plan in comparison to other health care facilities.	1	2	3	?
10. I would encourage someone to apply for work here.	1	2	3	?

Comments on 6–10: _____

Figure 2-10. This sample form shows an "opinionnaire" to be completed by staff to gather feedback on how well an organization's mission is implemented in its operations.

Source: McGuire TP, Longo BW: Evaluating your mission: A practical approach to developing and assessing a facility's organizational culture. *QRB,* Feb 1993, pp 51–52. Used with permission of Terrance P. McGuire, EdD, and Brother Warren Longo, CFA, of Alexian Brothers Health System, Inc, Elk Grove Village, Illinois.

FIGURE 2-10 (CONTINUED)
MISSION EFFECTIVENESS OPINIONNAIRE

	Low	Moderate	High	Don't Know
11. The pastoral care staff are readily available to be of service to patients, families, and employees.	1	2	3	?
12. The spiritual and pastoral counseling needs of patients are responded to in a prompt manner by pastoral care staff.	1	2	3	?
13. Attention is given to creating a working environment which actively fosters mutual cooperation among employees.	1	2	3	?
14. The Alexian Spirit Committee sponsors and supports facility activities that encourage a spirit of teamwork and foster the Alexian Spirit.	1	2	3	?
15. In-service programs and/or retreat experiences are offered to employees throughout the year.	1	2	3	?

Comments on 11–15: _____

	Low	Moderate	High	Don't Know
16. Your experience or knowledge tells you that quality health care is provided for patients of this facility.	1	2	3	?
17. Patients are treated with respect and dignity.	1	2	3	?
18. Family members of patients are treated courteously and with respect.	1	2	3	?
19. Patients are clearly advised of their rights and responsibilities.	1	2	3	?
20. By choice, I would choose to receive care in this facility.	1	2	3	?

Comments on 16–20: _____

	Low	Moderate	High	Don't Know
21. This facility provides quality care to patients regardless of their ability to pay for services.	1	2	3	?
22. The publications of the facility reflect in them the facility's mission.	1	2	3	?
23. I feel this facility responds to the health needs of the local community as they are identified.	1	2	3	?
24. I feel this facility is progressive in its delivery of health care services.	1	2	3	?
25. I would recommend this facility to other persons for their health care needs.	1	2	3	?

Comments on 21–25: _____

Please hand in completed opinionnaire at this time.

FIGURE 2-11
EMPOWERMENT SELF-ASSESSMENT

For each pair of phrases, circle the number that most closely indicates your usual behavior. Five and one represent the two extremes, while three represents middle ground.

Do you... | | | | | | **Or do you...**

Do you...						Or do you...
Seek input from others who will be affected by your decision?	5	4	3	2	1	Make decisions independent of others' input?
Regularly, openly, and systematically share information?	5	4	3	2	1	Closely guard or withhold information from others?
Confront others assertively but humanely?	5	4	3	2	1	Consistently avoid confrontation with others?
Take personal risks to solve problems?	5	4	3	2	1	Give in easily rather than take a risk?
Negotiate mutually acceptable resolutions to problems?	5	4	3	2	1	Take a position and maintain it at all costs?
Recognize and value individual differences in people?	5	4	3	2	1	Expect others to conform to your personal standards?
Treat everyone with equal dignity and respect?	5	4	3	2	1	Show favoritism to preferred individuals?
Accept constructive criticism?	5	4	3	2	1	Reject negative feedback from others?
Fulfill commitments made, even when they are very difficult?	5	4	3	2	1	Accept any barrier as an excuse to renege on commitment?
Suggest/support positive change?	5	4	3	2	1	Always work hard to maintain the status quo?
Defend the rights of others?	5	4	3	2	1	Disregard the rights of others?
Keep confidences scrupulously?	5	4	3	2	1	Reveal confidences indiscriminately?
Provide accurate information even if it is personally damaging?	5	4	3	2	1	Provide biased information?
Volunteer your true feelings, even when they may be unpopular?	5	4	3	2	1	Adopt as your own the opinion of the majority?
Make yourself visible and accessible?	5	4	3	2	1	Avoid contact with others?
Inspire others with positive enthusiasm?	5	4	3	2	1	Discourage others with negative comments and skepticism?

Scoring: 64–80 indicates a high level of empowerment.
48–63 indicates an average level of empowerment.
47 or lower indicates a low level of empowerment.

Figure 2-11. This assessment tool can be used by staff to determine how empowered they feel in their jobs.

Source: Adapted from Memorial Hospital of South Bend, Nursing Department, South Bend, IN. Used with permission.

FIGURE 2-12
COMMITMENT WORKSHEET

1. My definition of CQI is:

_____

_____

_____

_____

_____

2. How will CQI affect my behavior at work? Give examples:

_____

_____

_____

_____

_____

3. Give an example of a behavior that expresses one of your organization's values:

_____

_____

_____

_____

_____

4. What I need to be successful at CQI:

_____

_____

_____

_____

5. What I will do to make CQI "happen":

_____

_____

_____

_____

_____

Figure 2-12. This worksheet poses open-ended questions designed to help individuals understand their attitude toward and role in continuous quality improvement (CQI).

Source: © Organizational Learning Group, Mount Pleasant, South Carolina, 1993.

FIGURE 2–13
COST OF PERFORMANCE WORKSHEET

Department _____ **Date:** _____

Internal Failure Costs

Description [1]	No. hours per month [2]	$ Rate per hour [3]	$ Labor per month [4] [2] × [3]	$ Supply per month [5]	$ Other expenses per month [6]	$ Qual cost per month [7] [4] + [5] + [6]	$ Qual cost per year [8] [7] × 12
_____	_____	_____	_____	_____	_____	_____	_____
_____	_____	_____	_____	_____	_____	_____	_____
_____	_____	_____	_____	_____	_____	_____	_____
_____	_____	_____	_____	_____	_____	_____	_____
_____	_____	_____	_____	_____	_____	_____	_____
_____	_____	_____	_____	_____	_____	_____	_____
_____	_____	_____	_____	_____	_____	_____	_____
Total	_____	_____	_____	_____	_____	_____	_____

Department _____ **Date:** _____

External Failure Costs

Description [1]	No. hours per month [2]	$ Rate per hour [3]	$ Labor per month [4] [2] × [3]	$ Supply per month [5]	$ Other expenses per month [6]	$ Qual cost per month [7] [4] + [5] + [6]	$ Qual cost per year [8] [7] × 12
_____	_____	_____	_____	_____	_____	_____	_____
_____	_____	_____	_____	_____	_____	_____	_____
_____	_____	_____	_____	_____	_____	_____	_____
_____	_____	_____	_____	_____	_____	_____	_____
_____	_____	_____	_____	_____	_____	_____	_____
_____	_____	_____	_____	_____	_____	_____	_____
Total	_____	_____	_____	_____	_____	_____	_____

Figure 2-13. This form is used to measure costs associated with performance of a particular process prior to improvement.

Source: Reprinted from Daigh RD: Financial implications of a quality improvement process. *Topics in Health Care Financing* 17(3): 47–48, 1991, with permission of Aspen Publishers, Inc, © 1991.

FIGURE 2–13 (CONTINUED)
COST OF PERFORMANCE WORKSHEET

Department _____ **Date:** _____

Prevention Costs

Description [1]	No. hours per month [2]	$ Rate per hour [3]	$ Labor per month [4] [2] x [3]	$ Supply per month [5]	$ Other expenses per month [6]	$ Qual cost per month [7] [4] + [5] + [6]	$ Qual cost per year [8] [7] x 12
Total							

Department _____ **Date:** _____

Appraisal Costs

Description [1]	No. hours per month [2]	$ Rate per hour [3]	$ Labor per month [4] [2] x [3]	$ Supply per month [5]	$ Other expenses per month [6]	$ Qual cost per month [7] [4] + [5] + [6]	$ Qual cost per year [8] [7] x 12
Total							

FIGURE 2-14
EXAMPLES OF FORMS TO DOCUMENT CURRENT INFORMATION MANAGEMENT ACTIVITIES AS PART OF DESIGNING NEW SYSTEMS

Health Information Management Survey—Work Flow Requirements
Reviewed: _____

General Hospital Description

Name/Address: _____

Type of Hospital: _____

Primary Services: _____

Number of Beds: _____

Key Personnel

Primary Contact:	_____	Date:	_____
Administration:	_____	Date:	_____
Health Information:	_____	Date:	_____
Data Processing:	_____	Date:	_____

Staffing Levels in Medical Records

Total full-time personnel _____

Total part-time personnel _____

Task	# Full-time	# Part-time
Chart intake	_____	_____
Assembly	_____	_____
Deficiency analysis	_____	_____
Deficiency reinspection	_____	_____
Coding	_____	_____
Filing	_____	_____
Loose reports	_____	_____

Figure 2-14. If an organization is designing a new system, it is important to document current needs for such a system. These examples show how an organization planning to switch to optical disk technology documented information management needs so vendors could recommend the appropriate system.

Source: Rollins P: Converting to an optical disk system. *Topics in Health Information Management* 13(3): 40–44, 1993. Used with permission of Aspen Publishers, Inc.

FIGURE 2-14 (CONTINUED)
EXAMPLES OF FORMS TO DOCUMENT

Task	# Full-time	# Part-time
Chart tracking	_____	_____
Runners	_____	_____
Utilization review	_____	_____
Quality improvement	_____	_____
Correspondence	_____	_____
Medical transcription	_____	_____
Outpatient processing	_____	_____
Microfilming	_____	_____
Receptionist	_____	_____
Secretary	_____	_____
Birth certificates	_____	_____
Management	_____	_____

Patient Forms	# of sides per document
Face sheet	_____
Discharge summary	_____
History	_____
Physical examination	_____
Progress notes	_____
Consultations	_____
Physician orders	_____
Consent to treatment	_____
Anesthesia report	_____
Operative report	_____
Pathology report	_____
Laboratory reports	_____
Radiology reports	_____
Cardiology reports	_____
Therapy	_____
Social work	_____
Nursing forms	_____
Financial forms	_____
Other	_____

FIGURE 2-14 (CONTINUED)
EXAMPLES OF FORMS TO DOCUMENT

Indicate % of Records That Are: %

Handwritten notes   _____

Typewritten notes   _____

Matrix printed forms   _____

Lab mount sheets   _____

Strip EKGs   _____

Full-page EKGs   _____

Computer-generated and computer source   _____

Total of above should equal 100%   _____

% of above that is character-based DP/WP* generated   _____

Filing/Refiling (Completed Records)

Number of records filed/refiled: _____

Indicated % for each type of retrieval: _____

   Scheduled outpatient   _____

   Scheduled inpatient   _____

   Emergency   _____

   Quality inspection/utilization review   _____

   Physician request   _____

   Correspondence   _____

   Audit   _____

   Total   100%

Correspondence

Copy requests:

   From paper   _____

   From film   _____

   From fiche   _____

*DP/WP=data processing/word processing

CUSTOMER ANALYSIS AND SURVEY TOOLS

These tools can help an organization identify its key customers
and gather performance-related information from those customers
(especially patients).

FIGURE 3-1
CUSTOMER WORKSHEET

Customers	Immediate/ Ultimate Expectations	Expectancy Level			Measure
		Assumed	Requested	Delighted	

Figure 3-1. This worksheet helps staff identify customer needs and expectations for a given process. For each process, staff identify their customers and the immediate and ultimate expectations of each customer group. The worksheet then directs staff to assign a level—"assumed," "requested," or "delighted"—to each expectation. "Assumed" is a foundational expectation. For example, patients admitted as inpatients to a hospital assume they will have a bed and see a nurse and doctor. "Requested" expectations indicate a higher degree of customer specifications. For example, patients expect courtesy and short waiting times. Finally, a customer is "delighted" when service exceeds the "requested" level. The patient might be delighted if he or she has no paperwork to complete or sees a doctor without any wait. Finally, the worksheet asks staff to identify measures for some or all of the needs and expectations. The results of this worksheet help ensure that measurement, assessment, and improvement pay attention to customers.

Source: West Paces Medical Center, Atlanta, GA, 1992. Used with permission.

FIGURE 3-2
CUSTOMER EXPECTATIONS MATRICES

Customer Groups (CG)

CG \ CE	High Quality	Low Cost	Accessible	Know What to Expect	Easy to Understand	Seamless	Functionality	Customer Expectations (CE) # STRONG
PATIENTS	■	◪	■	■	◪	□	■	④*
PAYERS	◪	■	□	□	□	□	◪	1
PT. FAMILIES	■	□	■	■	□	□	■	⑤
PHYSICIANS	■	◪	◪	□	□	□	◪	1
REGULATORY	■	◪	◪	■	□	◪	◪	1
# STRONG	④	1	2	2	1	0	2	

Customer Expectations (CE)

CE \ BS	Documentation	Standing Orders	Preference Cards	Care Plans	Education	Satisfaction	Concurent Data	Key Quality Charactersitics	Business Strategies (BS) # STRONG
HIGH QUALITY	■	■	■	■	■	■	■	■	⑧
LOW COST	◪	■	■	■	◪	◪	◪	■	4
ACCESSIBLE	□	□	□	◪	■	■	□	□	2
KNOW WHAT TO EXPECT	◪	■	◪	■	■	■	□	□	4
EASY TO UNDERSTAND	◪	■	□	■	■	■	□	□	4
SEAMLESS	■	◪	□	■	■	◪	■	□	4
FUNCTIONALITY	■	◪	□	■	■	■	□	□	4
# STRONG	3	4	2	⑥	⑥	5	2	2	

* Circled numbers represent the strongest relationships.

Figure 3-2. These two matrices demonstrate one method for gauging customer expectations. In the first matrix, customer expectations are weighed against customer groups. In the second matrix, business strategies are weighed against customer expectations. The square indicates the strength of the relationship (empty=weak; full=strong).

Source: QI keys identified to ensure hospital supports physicians, clinical paths. *QI/TQM* 4(2): 14–15, 1994. Used with permission of Parkview Episcopal Medical Center, Pueblo, CO.

FIGURE 3-3
STAKEHOLDER ANALYSIS

Vision: Reduce staff in account payable function by at least 75%			
Future States	**Areas of Change**	**Changes**	**Key Stakeholders**
Pay on receipt instead of on invoice	Process	• Design new process	• Accounts payable • Receive and inspect • Information system
	Technology	• Build common database for plants and payables	• Information systems
	Organization/culture	• Restructure jobs and retrain staff • Manage staff redeployments	• Plant management • Financial management • Personnel • Union

				Commitment						
				Capability	Readiness	Level				
Stakeholder	**Change Needed**	**Perceived Benefits**	**Perceived Resistance**	**(low, medium, high)**	**(low, medium, high)**	**None**	**Let it Happen**	**Help it Happen**	**Make it Happen**	**Recommended Actions**
• Plant management • Financial management • Personnel • Union	• Restructure jobs • Retrain staff • Manage redeployment	• Large manpower savings	• Loss of control • Doubts about project feasibility • Distaste for managing redeployment	High	Low	X (present level)			→○ (necessary level)	• Show necessity • Indicate rewards • Prototype

Figure 3-3. A stakeholder analysis is a tool to manage a process or product redesign. The chart identifies parties who have some stake in the change, the perceived benefits and resistance on the part of the stakeholders, and the stakeholders' level of committment to the change.

Source: Reprinted from Benjamin RI, Levinson E: A framework for managing IT-enabled change. *Sloan Management Review* pp 30–31, Summer 1993 ©1993, by permission of publisher, Sloan Management Review Association. All rights reserved.

FIGURE 3-4
CUSTOMER ANALYSIS MATRIX

Customers	Quality Characteristic					Total
	Education	Budget	Costs	Length of Stay	Quality of Care	
Patients						
Physicians						
Nursing staff						
Health care employees						
Government						
Insurance companies						
Public						

Key:
3—Heavy Effect
2—Moderate Effect
1—Light Effect
0—No Effect

Figure 3-4. This matrix can be used to analyze how an organization's different groups of customers affect a variety of "quality characteristics," such as costs and lengths of stay. To complete this matrix, rank each customer's effect on each characteristic as heavy, moderate, light, or none, and total the results in the column on the right.

Source: Adapted from Gopalakrishnan KN, McIntryre BE: Hurdles to quality health care. *Quality Progress,* Apr 1992, p 94.

FIGURE 3-5
PHARMACY CONTROL PLAN

Department: Pharmacy

Function	Customers	Expectations/ requirements	Quality indicator	Quality standard	Measurement tool	Outcome evaluation	Action	Results	Report
Responsible for optimal drug therapy	Patient	Resolve problems as simply and as soon as possible	Number of DTM interventions per patient	Baseline from first 1,100 interventions	DTM form	Graphic			Monthly
		Expect medication won't worsen/ make sicker	Type of DTM intervention	Baseline from first 1,100 interventions	DTM form	Graphic			Monthly
		No harm	Quality ranking of DTM intervention or risk indicator	Baseline from first 1,100 interventions	DTM form	Graphic			Monthly

Figure 3-5. This plan promotes a consistent definition of customer needs and expectations within a pharmacy service.

Source: Adapted from Owad WP Jr.; Developing a customer-driven approach to quality improvement systems. *Topics in Hospital Pharmacy Management* 12(4): 68, 1993. ©1992 American Society for Quality Control. Used with permission of Toledo Hospital, Toledo, OH.

FIGURE 3-6
PATIENT SURVEY TOOL

CENTRAL HOSPICE CARE

WE NEED YOUR HELP!

It may be painful to think back to the time when the hospice team members were frequently visitors to your home, but we need you to help us make sure that we are providing the services our families need. Please take a moment or two to answer a few questions and rate our performance. We have enclosed a stamped, addressed envelope for your convenience.

• How satisfied were you with what we taught you about taking care of your loved one?

1 _____	2 _____	3 _____	4 _____	5 _____
extremely	very	satisfied	not very	not at all

• How satisfied were you that we visited you when you needed us?

1 _____	2 _____	3 _____	4 _____	5 _____
extremely	very	satisfied	not very	not at all

• How satisfied were you with our equipment service?

1 _____	2 _____	3 _____	4 _____	5 _____
extremely	very	satisfied	not very	not at all

• How satisfied were you with our medication service?

1 _____	2 _____	3 _____	4 _____	5 _____
extremely	very	satisfied	not very	not at all

• How satisfied were you with our personal care service?

1 _____	2 _____	3 _____	4 _____	5 _____
extremely	very	satisfied	not very	not at all

• How satisfied were you that the patient's pain was controlled?

1 _____	2 _____	3 _____	4 _____	5 _____
extremely	very	satisfied	not very	not at all

• How satisfied were you with our team members' courtesy/politeness?

1 _____	2 _____	3 _____	4 _____	5 _____
extremely	very	satisfied	not very	not at all

Comments _____

Would you recommend our services to a friend in need?   Yes _____   No _____

Signature (optional) _____

Please list your phone number if you would like someone to call you. _____

Thank you for your help.

Figure 3-6. This is an example of a survey tool to garner patient feedback that can be used in quality improvement activities.

Source: Central Hospice Care, Atlanta, GA, 1992. Used with permission.

FIGURE 3-7
QUESTIONNAIRE FOR PARTICIPANTS

Directions: Please read each statement in the first column below. Consider how you felt about this statement after completion of the six-week Childbirth Preparation Series at Akron General Medical Center. Put a checkmark in the response column that most closely matches your feelings. Please remember that each statement should have only one checkmark in the response columns.

Statement	Response				
	Strongly agree	Agree	Not sure	Disagree	Strongly disagree
1. I understood what "family centered care" meant.					
2. I understood some causes and ways to relieve common discomforts of pregnancy.					
3. I knew what an appropriate diet during pregnancy should consist of.					
4. I knew the importance of good dental care during pregnancy and why.					
5. I knew the difference between true and false labor.					
6. I knew how I could assess the difference between true and false labor.					
7. I knew some possible causes of labor.					
8. I knew the stages of labor.					
9. I knew what to expect during the various stages of labor. I knew what "early labor" meant.					
10. I knew some exercises I could perform to "warm up" my muscles, tone my muscles, and strengthen my pelvic muscles.					
11. I knew methods of active relaxation. I knew appropriate breathing techniques that are to be used during labor.					
12. I knew reasons for some prenatal tests and what happens during the performance of the test, including the following: amniocentesis and					

Figure 3-7. This questionnaire measures satisfaction with a six-week childbirth education class.

Source: Finks HH, et al: An outcome evaluation of a six-week childbirth education class. *Journal of Nursing Care Quality* 7(3): 78–81, 1993. Used with permission of Karol H. Klark, MSN, RNC, Akron General Medical Center (OH); Hollis H. Finks, MSN, DN, Ashland University School of Nursing; Diane S. Hill, MSN, RNC, St Elizabeth School of Nursing.

FIGURE 3-7 (CONTINUED)
QUESTIONNAIRE FOR PARTICIPANTS

	Response				
Statement	**Strongly agree**	**Agree**	**Not sure**	**Disagree**	**Strongly disagree**
13. ultrasound.					
14. I knew what "active labor" meant and what to expect during this period of labor.					
15. I knew some of the common hospital procedures during labor and what to expect.					
16. I understood how my labor might be induced or stimulated if necessary.					
17. I knew danger signs I should be aware of during pregnancy that would indicate the need for me to contact my physician or go to the emergency department.					
18. I knew what "back labor" meant and some possible ways to ease the pain.					
19. I knew what "transition" meant and what to expect during that phase of labor.					
20. I knew methods of anesthesia and the differences between the various types.					
21. I knew what to do during the "pushing" phase of labor and how this could be best accomplished.					
22. I knew reasons why a cesarean section may need to be performed.					
23. I knew what to expect if a cesarean section was performed.					
24. I knew what to expect my baby to look like at birth.					
25. I knew the different positions my baby may "present" (that is, breech, face, shoulder).					
26. I knew how these various presentations could affect my delivery.					

FIGURE 3-7 (CONTINUED)
QUESTIONNAIRE FOR PARTICIPANTS

Statement	Response				
	Strongly agree	Agree	Not sure	Disagree	Strongly disagree
27. I knew what to expect during my initial recovery period after delivery.					
28. I knew what to expect during my postpartum recovery and how I would care for myself in the following areas: breast care,					
29. perineal care,					
30. incisional care,					
31. emotional care,					
32. nutrition, and					
33. adequate rest.					
34. I knew how to care for my baby after delivery as follows: umbilical cord care,					
35. bathing,					
36. diapering,					
37. safety,					
38. bottle feeding,					
39. breastfeeding, and					
40. dressing my baby.					
41. I knew the importance of having a will.					

Who was your childbirth educator? _____

What was your due date? _____

What day did you deliver?_____ How much did the baby weigh? _____

Did you have a boy or girl? _____

Did your have a vaginal or cesarean delivery? _____

Are you breastfeeding or formula feeding? _____

Was there anything that you were taught in the classes that was not important to you? (If yes, please describe)

_____

Please list information that was not taught that you think should be included in childbirth education classes.

_____

_____

Any other comments are welcome. _____

FIGURE 3-8
QUALITY OF CARE QUESTIONNAIRE

**Baltimore County Department of Health
Public Health Nursing Services**

Date _____   Time Started Interview _____
Interviewer _____   Time Completed Interview _____

Healthy Start Patient Input and Outcome Questionnaire

Hello! My name is _____ from the Baltimore County Department of Health. I am calling randomly selected patients to determine whether we are providing good patient care services in the home. This survey will take only five minutes, is voluntary and in no way affects your care. Would you be willing to participate?

1. Has a public health nurse visited you at your home?
    Yes _____
    No _____ Thank you for your time! this survey concerns our home visiting services only.

    Only continue if the patient said "Yes" to the above question.

2. How many visits have you received from the public health nurse?
    Only 1 _____
    2 _____
    3 _____
    4 _____
    More than 4 _____

3. Did you feel these nursing visits were useful?
    Yes _____
    No _____

4. In any of these visits, did the nurse discuss the importance of keeping prenatal appointments with you?
    Yes _____
    No _____
    Don't know _____

Figure 3-8. This questionnaire was used by a phone interviewer to determine whether the Baltimore County Department of Health was providing good home care services to patients.

Source: Zlotnick C, Gould P: Prenatal quality of life outcomes for a public health quality assurance system. *Journal of Nursing Care Quality* 7(3): 43–45, 1993. Used with permission of Baltimore County Department of Health, Public Health Nursing Services, © 1991.

FIGURE 3-8 (CONTINUED)
QUALITY OF CARE QUESTIONNAIRE

5. Do you have difficulties keeping these prenatal appointments?

         Yes _____
          No _____
    Don't know _____

6. During the public health nurses visit, did he or she talk to you about the Woman, Infants, and Children or WIC program?

         Yes _____ ——————————→ 6A. Are you enrolled in the program?
          No _____   Yes _____
    Don't know _____   No _____
                                              Don't know _____

                                      6B. Did you find it difficult to get into the program?
                                                Yes _____
                                                 No _____
                                           Don't know _____

7. Do you feel you are eating well?

         Yes _____
          No _____
    Don't know _____

8. Do you feel your health is good?

         Yes _____
          No _____
    Don't know _____

9. Did the nurse discuss with you the danger signs of premature labor?

         Yes _____ ——————————→ 9A. Did you feel comfortable asking the nurse questions?
          No _____   Yes _____
    Don't know _____   No _____
                                              Don't know _____

                                      9B. Was the information that the nurse gave you easy to understand?
                                                Yes _____
                                                 No _____
                                           Don't know _____

10. Do you feel safe and secure in your Baltimore County neighborhood?

         Yes _____
          No _____
    Don't know _____

FIGURE 3-8 (CONTINUED)
QUALITY OF CARE QUESTIONNAIRE

11. Do you feel that you are able to get the services you need for your pregnancy?

        Yes _____

         No _____

Don't know _____

               What services do you feel you need that are unavailable?

               _____

               _____

12. Do you feel that you have all the information you need to care for your baby?

        Yes _____

         No _____

Don't know _____

               What additional information would you like to receive?

               _____

               _____

               Would you like me to have a nurse call you and provide some additional information?

               _____

               _____

13. Are you worried about getting pediatric services for your child, once he or she is born?

        Yes _____   Mention that Baltimore County does provide well-child services.

         No _____

Don't know _____

14. Do you feel you have the help you need from your family and friends?

        Yes _____

         No _____

Don't know _____   Would you like me to have a nurse call you about this? _____

15. Is there any information you would like to add that would help us provide better prenatal care and/or home visits?

_____

_____

_____

_____

Thank you for participating in this survey!

FLOWCHARTS

Flowcharts help document current processes, redesign current processes, and design new processes. This section presents several different types of flowcharts.

FIGURE 4-1
MATRIX FLOWCHART

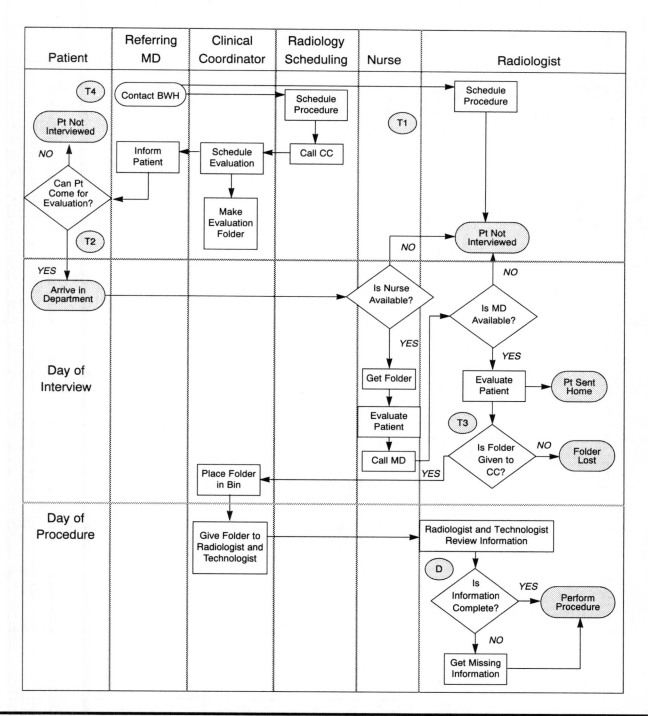

Figure 4-1. This matrix flowchart of the process for performing patient evaluations prior to cardiovascular and interventional radiology procedures was used as an aid in generating theories regarding the cause of missed evaluations. Theories are labeled "T1", "T2", "T3", and "T4". These theories were tested by establishing a data collection effort at the point marked D. (Pt=patient; MD=physician; CC=clinic coordinator.)

Source: Chopra PS, et al: Improving the patient evaluation process in a cardiovascular and interventional radiology department. *Quality Management in Health Care* 1(1):23, 1992. Used with permission of Aspen Publishers, Inc.

FIGURE 4-2
DEPLOYMENT FLOWCHART: PREPARING FOR HOSPITAL ADMISSION

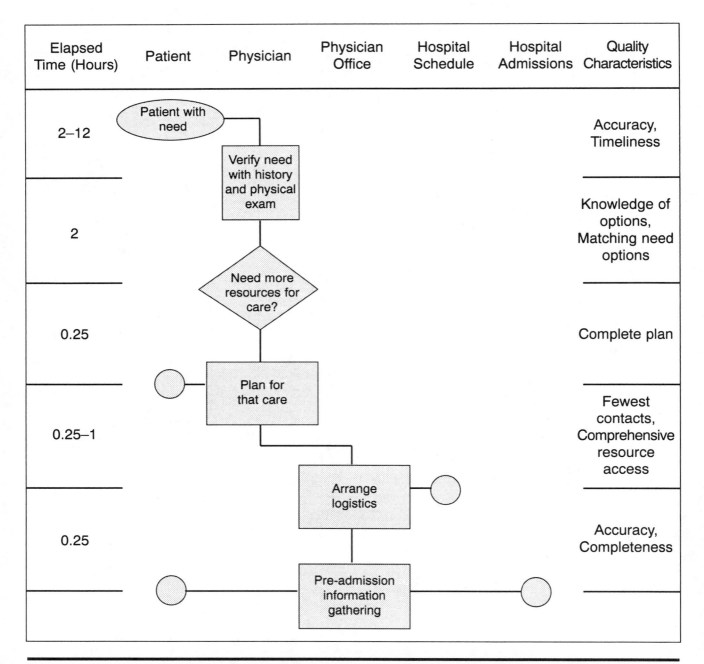

Figure 4-2. A particularly helpful type of flowchart is the deployment flowchart. This example shows a portion of the process of preparing for hospital admission. The process steps are arranged by key player and site. Elapsed time for various steps is shown in the left margin, and the quality characteristics most important to customers are shown for each step in the right margin.

Source: Batalden PB, Stoltz PK: A framework for the continual improvement of health care: Building and applying professional and improvement knowledge to test changes in daily work. *The Joint Commission Journal on Quality Improvement* 19(10): 435, 1993. © 1993, Joint Commission on Accreditation of Healthcare Organizations.

FIGURE 4-3
TOP-DOWN PROCESS FLOWCHART

1. Registration	2. Posting/ Invoicing	3. Processing Statements	4. Processing Insurance Forms	5. Monitoring Accounts
1.1 New client receives registration materials 1.1.1 Staff reviews forms—are they complete? 1.1.2 Forms to clinician 1.2 Client seen by clinician 1.3 Clinician discusses fee structure/payment plan 1.3.1 Obtain final signature 1.4 All materials back to staff to complete registration process	2.1 Staff prepares posting sheets daily with client name/account number/date 2.2 Clinicians receive client chart and posting sheet 2.3 Clinicians enter charges/procedure codes on posting sheets 2.4 Clinician returns posting sheets to staff 2.5 Staff totals charges and batches 2.6 Posting sheets to data entry	3.1 Registration/ charge data entered on-line to billing service 3.2 Statements produced monthly on alpha cycle	4.1 Insurance forms produced monthly on alpha cycle 4.2 Claims signed and mailed	5.1 Clinicians review delinquent balance sheets monthly 5.2 Clinicians forward concerns to staff for review 5.3 Staff meets with clinicians to review personal and insurance payments 5.4 Staff recommends action on accounts 5.5 Personal contact with client
Client recalled to fill out registration materials Clinician recontacted to gather more account information	Staff translates clinician "short-hand" in appointment book Staff locates missing information Staff adds any missing information	Clinician recontacted to verify fee/monthly payments Staff finds documents to support adjustments to postings Staff responds to client questions/ posting errors Staff gathers and verifies corrected information Staff manually corrects/adjusts accounts	Claims audited for accuracy Errors corrected before sending to insurance carrier Procedure codes corrected as necessary	

Figure 4-3. The top-down flowchart illustrates the major steps of a process in a simple, horizontal flowchart, with substeps listed beneath the appropriate major step. This chart has several benefits: it allows the major steps of a process to be readily identified, it shows the relative complexity of the different steps in a process, and it allows substeps to be added easily. This example illustrates processing patient accounts at a clinic.

Source: Affiliated Psychological Resources, Madison, WI, 1993.

FIGURE 4-4
QUICK MAPS OF PROCESS IMPROVEMENT

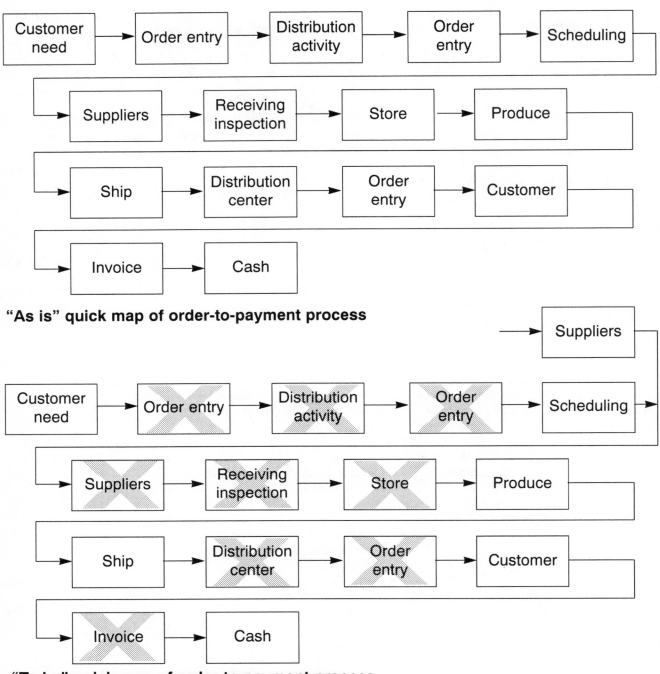

"As is" quick map of order-to-payment process

**"To be" quick map of order-to-payment process
after the BreakPoint BPR℠ process**

Figure 4-4. An "as is" quick map (a simplified flowchart) traces the existing steps involved in a process (in this case, order to payment). The "to be" quick map shows which steps can be streamlined out of the process.

Source: Carr DK, Littman ID: Getting the breaks. *The TQM Magazine*, Nov–Dec 1993, p 62.

FIGURE 4-5
CORE PROCESS AND SUPPORT PROCESS MAP

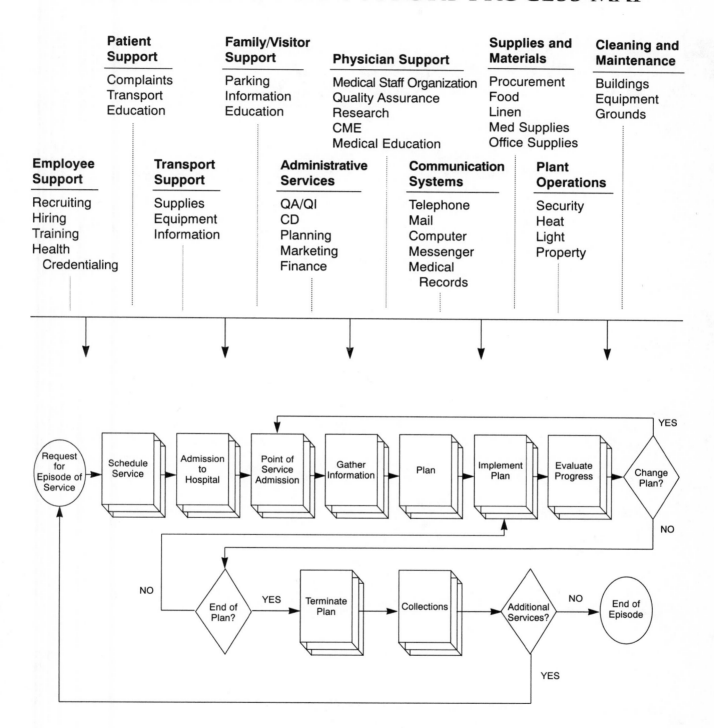

Figure 4-5. This map shows the linkage of processes that come together to provide a service for a patient. Such a map offers health care workers a fresh perspective on the system of their work and allows workers and leaders to visualize their interdependencies.

Source: Ferguson S, et al: Knowledge and skills needed for collaborative work. *Quality Management in Health Care* 1(2): 4, 1993. Reprinted with permission from Jim Biltz, President, CEO, HCA Wesley Medical Center, Wichita, KS.

CRITICAL
PATHS

Critical paths guide basic treatment procedures for select diagnoses as a way to eliminate unnecessary variation. This section presents various formats and uses of this tool.

FIGURE 5-1 (A)
CRITICAL PATH: UNCOMPLICATED
CORONARY ARTERY BYPASS

	PAT Date Day of Week	OPS/DOS Date Day of Week	OR/DOS Date Day of Week	ICU/DOS Date Day of Week
Assessments Evaluations	Nursing assessment ___ Anesthesia assessment ___ Inter H&P or letter ___ Chart requirements met ___ Consent ___ Admission note ___	Nursing assessment ___ SDA/OPS 0530-0600 ___ Anesthesia assessment ___ Chart requirements met ___	Nursing assessment ___ Chart requirements met ___ Anesthesia assessment ongoing ___	Nursing assessment 7–3 ___ 3–11 ___ 11–7 ___ RT assessment ___ Post-op VS till stable ___ VS protocol ___

Tests	Routine UA ___
	EKG ___
	Chest x-ray (PA & LAT) ___
	Chem 20, CBC, PTT,
	  PT, Plt count ___
	Type & cross 4
	  units/6 units ___
	Pregnancy test if ind. ___
			ABG's ongoing ___
			Heart profile: RBS, LTYES, Ca,
			  Hgb, Hct ___
			Co-Oximetry ___
				Chest x-ray ___
				EKG ___
				ABG, CBC, CUN, Cr,
				PT, PTT, CPK, LDH,
				Isos ___

Consults	Confirm medical
	  evaluation complete ___
				Pulmonary Cardiology
				  Co-manage ___
				Cardiac Rehab ___

Treatments		Accurate height/weight ___ Shave/prep ___ Nasal O_2 ___	Insert PA catheter ___ Insert A-line ___ Apply cardiac monitor ___ Pulse oximetry ___ IABP standby ___ Intubate/ventilator ___ Prep ___ Drape ___ Surgery/bypass ___ Autotransfuser ___ Chest tubes ___ Pacer wires ___ Warming blanket ___ Dressings ___	Bed weight ___ Nurse initiated C&DB ___ Dressing assessed ___ Ventilator ___ RT treatments ___ Autotransfusion ___ Pulse oximetry ___ Hemodynamic monitoring ___ Chest tubes ___ Pacer standby ___ Warming blanket ___ Cardiac monitoring ___

Medications	Confirm availability of
	autologous blood if
	ordered ___
		Start 2 IV peripheral
		  lines ___
		Prophylactic antibiotic
		  pre-op ___
			Anesthesia sedation ___
			Blood therapy ___
				IV ___
				IV meds ___
				Vasopressors ___
				Post-op sedation ___

Activity		ABR ___	ABR ___	ABR Card Rehab passive ROM ___
Diet		NPO ___	NPO ___	NPO ___

Figure 5-1. This figure shows a two-part critical path form. One part, 5-1(A), shows a partial critical path for uncomplicated open heart surgery. The other part, 5-1(B), is the form for documenting any variance from the procedure.

Source: Hofmann PA: Critical path method: An important tool for coordinating clinical care, *The Joint Commission Journal on Quality Improvement* 19(7): 239–240, 1993. Used with permission of Mount Clements General Hospital's (Mount Clements, MI) cardiac surgeons, cardiologist, nursing staff, and TQM staff.

FIGURE 5-1 (A) (CONTINUED)
CRITICAL PATH: UNCOMPLICATED
CORONARY ARTERY BYPASS

	PO Day 1 Date Day of Week	PO Day 2 Date Day of Week	PO Day 3 Date Day of Week	PO Day 4 Date Day of Week	PO Day 5 Date Day of Week
Assessments Evaluations	Nursing Assessment 7–3 ___ 3–11 ___ 11–7 ___ RT assessment ___ Nutritional screen ___ VS protocol ___	Nursing Assessment 7–3 ___ 3–11 ___ 11–7 ___ VS protocol ___	Nursing Assessment 7–3 ___ 3–11 ___ 11–7 ___ VS protocol ___	Nursing Assessment 7–3 ___ 3–11 ___ 11–7 ___ VS protocol ___	Nursing Assessment 7–3 ___ 3–11 ___ 11–7 ___ VS protocol ___

Tests	Pre/post extubation
	ABG's ___
	CBC, BUN, Cr, LYTES,
	  CPK, LDH, SGOT,
	  PT, PTT, Plt count ___
	EKG ___
	Chest x-ray ___
		EKG ___
		CBC, BUN, Cr, LYTES,
		  CPK, LDH, SGOT,
		  PT, PTT, Plt count ___
		Chest x-ray ___
			EKG ___
			CBC, LTYES ___
			Chest x-ray ___		

Consults	Pulmonary rehab ___				

Treatments	Wean/extubate within
	  12 hours ___
	Incentive spirometry ___
	Chest physical therapy ___
	Weight 06:00 ___
	O$_2$ therapy ___
	Dressing changes ___
	Cough & deep breathe ___
	Cardiac monitoring ___
		Pulse oximetry prn ___
		Weight 0:600 ___
		Incision checks ___
		DC dsg prior to transfer ___
		Assess for DC
		  chest tubes
		  pacer lines ___
		Cardiac monitoring ___
		O$_2$ therapy per RT
		  protocol ___
			Weight 06:00 ___
			Incision checks ___
			Cardiac monitoring ___
			O$_2$ therapy per RT
			  protocol ___
				Weight 06:00 ___
				Incision checks ___
				Cardiac monitoring ___
					Weight 06:00 ___
					Incision checks ___
					Cardiac monitoring ___

Medications	IV ___ IV pain meds ___ Blood therapy ___ Vasopressor ___ Post-op sedation ___	IM to PO pain RX ___ DC IV lines main 1 peripheral IV ___ Routine meds ___	Routine meds ___ Change to heplock ___ PO meds ___	Routine meds ___ DC heplock ___ PO meds ___	Routine meds ___ PO meds ___
Activity	Up in chair ___ Cardiac rehab ___ Pulmonary rehab ___	Amb in room with assistance ___ Cardiac rehab ___ Pulmonary rehab ___	Amb in hall ___ Cardiac rehab ___	Amb in hall ___ Cardiac rehab/TM ___	Amb in hall ___ Shower ___ Cardiac rehab/TM ___
Diet	Cl. liq p extubation ___ Prog to 4 gm Na AHA low cholesterol ___	4 gm Na AHA ___	4 gm Na AHA ___	4 gm Na AHA ___	4 gm Na AHA ___

FIGURE 5-1 (B)
CRITICAL PATH: UNCOMPLICATED
CORONARY ARTERY BYPASS

**Critical Path:
Uncomplicated
Open Heart Surgery**

Variance Report

Date	Unit	Critical Path Day	Variance/Cause	Action	Signature

FIGURE 5-2
CRITICAL PATHWAY FOR TOTAL HIP REPLACEMENT (THR)

DRG 209   **Expected LOS: 7 days**

DEPARTMENT	Pre-Admit	Surgery	1	2
PREADMISSION	Orthopedist visit Internist visit Autologous blood donation x 3 Pre-admit clinic Outpatient social work			
ADMISSION		Admit 7 East 8th floor room		

MEDICATION ❶		Epidural analgesia ⟶
		Dextran w/Promit—start
		  preop
		Cefazolin 2 gm IV in holding ⟶
		  room, then as ordered by MD
		Intravenous ⟶
		Autologous blood reinfuse ⟶
				Oral analgesics

NUTRITION		NPO Clear fluids	Full liquids	Diet as tolerated
NURSING ACTIVITY		Complete bed rest—turn ⟶ every 2 hours		Ambulate with device

LABORATORY	Automated blood
	  count (ABC)
	PT/PTT
	Type/screen
	  autologous blood
			ABC ⟶	

RADIOLOGY		Hip x-ray (PACU)		
CONSULTS	Social work		Social work ⟶ PT (gait training)	
CENTRAL SUPPLY		Abduction pillow ⟶ Anti-embolic hose ⟶ Hemovac ⟶		
URINARY		Foley catheter ⟶		Straight catheter PRN Fracture pan
GASTROINTESTINAL				Bowel sounds
RESPIRATORY		Turn, cough, deep breathing ⟶		

EDUCATION ❷	THR precautions ⟶
	Pain control ⟶
				Pain control
				Use of assistive
				  device
				Gait training
				Sitting (including
				  automobile)

Figure 5-2. This figure shows a critical pathway. The format is amenable for many medical procedures; this example is for total hip replacement. The critical path tracks the course of a patient's total care from preadmission to discharge, thereby reducing patient-to-patient variations.

Source: Using critical pathways to develop standards of care, *The Quality Letter*, May 1992, pp 18-19. Used with permission of Sisters of Providence Health System, Portland, Oregon.

FIGURE 5-2 (CONTINUED)
CRITICAL PATHWAY FOR TOTAL HIP REPLACEMENT (THR)

3	4	5	6	Discharge Outcome
8th floor room ———————————→				
Epidural analgesia Oral analgesics ———————————→				Patient verbalizes dose, frequency, and side effects of analgesic Patient verbalizes pain, which is controlled with the use of oral analgesic prescribed at discharge (d/c)
				Patient is able to tolerate pre-admission diet
Ambulate with device ———————→	Bathroom privileges with standby assistance ————→			Patient is independent in ambulation with assistive device Skin is intact
	Automated blood count			Patient hemoglobin and hematocrit within normal limits
				No hip dislocation
Social work ————————————→ Home care ———————————————→ PT (gait training) ——————————→	OT (ADL training) —————————→		Discharge Day	D/c plan effective Patient d/c home with appropriate follow-up Patient independent in ambulation with assistive device Patient independent in ADLs with adaptive equipment
Abduction pillow ———————————→ Anti-embolic hose ——————————→		Dressing change		Patient takes home abduction pillow and anti-embolic hose
Fracture pan	Bathroom privileges with elevated seat ————————→			Patient voids qs on toilet with elevated seat
Bowel sounds	Bowel movement ————————→			Bowel tones auscultated in all quads Bowel movements return to preadmission schedule
	Turn, cough, deep breathing			Lungs clear to auscultation
THR precautions ——————————→ Pain control ————————————→ Use of assistive device ———————→ Gait training ——————————————→ Sitting (including automobile) ——→ S/S infection/DVT/ dislocation ——→ ADL ——————————————————→	Stairs —————————————————→			Patient verbalizes and demonstrates THR precautions, ambulation with use of walker/crutches, sitting, stairs, ADLs with adaptive devices, and getting in and out of automobile Patient verbalizes use of analgesia, s/s of infection/DVT/dislocation, d/c activity restrictions, use of anti-embolic hose and abduction pillow, and follow-up appointment with MD

PT = physical therapy
OT = occupational therapy

ADL = activities of daily living
S/S = signs and symptoms

QS = sufficient quantity

FIGURE 5-3
CRITICAL PATH WITH OUTCOME MEASURES

Collaborative Focus Areas; Add additional areas to individualize	Initial Patient/Family Outcomes	Intermediate Patient/Family Outcomes	Discharge (DC) Patient/Family Outcomes	Complete and Initial		
				Date Init. Met	Yes	No
			Record DC Date _____			
1. Alteration in cardiac output related to dysrhythmia	Patient will demonstrate clinical stability and absence of complications	Pacer will sense/capture correctly with appropriate rhythm for patient	Pacer sensing/ pacing appropriately			
			A febrile for 24 hrs prior to discharge			
			Patient back to baseline activity without dizziness			
			Incision intact without drainage or redness			
2. Knowledge deficit related to dysrhythmia/pacemaker	Patient/family verbalize their knowledge level and identify their learning needs	Patient/family verbalize understanding of meds and follow-up pacemaker care	Enrolled in Metro Cardiology Pacer clinic			
			Patient/significant other understand post-pacer instructions—follow-up care			
			Enrolled in Pacemaker Checking Program (Cardiocade)			
			Pacemaker ID card given			

Figure 5-3. This critical path format not only guides practitioners through the procedure (pacemaker insertion in this example), but also provides initial, intermediate, and discharge outcome measures and a format for documenting performance related to those measures.

FIGURE 5-3 (CONTINUED)
CRITICAL PATH WITH OUTCOME MEASURES

Anticipated Recovery Plan

* As indicated by physician
✓ Red check indicates MD order

Profile:

Case Type _PACEMAKER INSERTION_
DRG ____ Expected LOS _2_ days
Secondary Diagnosis _____
_____
Admission Date _____
Surgery Date _____

Physician _____
Consults _____
_____
_____
RN Initiated/Reviewed with Pt/family
_____

Name_____

Age _____

Rm#_____

Allergies (in Red)	Social History	Health History	Family/Emerg. Phone/Religion
Code Status / **Special Needs:** Visual _____ Hearing _____ Communication ___			

Staff Alert:
(use pencil)

Wt/Freq _____

Call If:
(use pencil)

Daily Labs:
(use pencil)

Therapy:
OT/PT/RC
(use pencil)

Living will: Y/N   In Chart: Y/N

COLLABORATIVE FOCUS AREAS ADD ADDITIONAL AREAS TO INDIVIDUALIZE	INITIAL PATIENT/FAMILY OUTCOMES	INTERMEDIATE PATIENT/FAMILY OUTCOMES	DISCHARGE PATIENT/FAMILY OUTCOMES	COMPLETE & INITIAL		
			RECORD DC DATE _____	Date initially met	Met at D/C Yes	No
1) Alteration in cardiac output related to dysrhythmia.	Patient will demonstrate clinical stability and absence of complications.	Pacer will sense/capture correctly with appropriate rhythm for patient.	Pacer sensing/pacing appropriately.			
			A febrile for 24 hrs. prior to discharge.			
			Patient back to baseline activity without dizziness.			
			Incision intact without drainage or redness.			
2) Knowledge deficit related to dysrhythmia/pacemaker.	Patient/family verbalize their knowledge level and identify their learning needs.	Patient/family verbalize understanding of meds and follow-up pacemaker care.	Enrolled in Metro Cardiology Pacer clinic.			
			Patient/significant other understand post pacer instructions—follow up care.			
			Enrolled in Pacemaker Checking Program (Cardiocade).			
			Pacemaker ID card given.			

SIGNATURE ON BACK

FIGURE 5-3 (CONTINUED)
CRITICAL PATH WITH OUTCOME MEASURES

Anticipated Recovery Plan (cont)

Case Type PACEMAKER INSERTION

	Day ___ADM___ Date _____	Day ___1___ Date _____	Day ___2___ Date _____	Day _____ Date _____	Day _____ Date _____
Nursing Assessment	Compile data and assess Telemetry ⟶		DC telemetry		
	Monitor for pacemaker sensing/capturing appropriately/proper rate				
	VS q 4 hrs after insertion	VS q shift	VS BID		
	Daily weight ⟶			⟶	
	Spotcheck O_2 saturation q shift ⟶			⟶	
			Assess ADLs	⟶	
	Assess comfort level and medicate as needed ⟶			⟶	
Treatments	Shoulder immobilizer to _____ arm ⟶			⟶	
IVS/Lines Medications* See medication record	Heplock	Heplock			
Activity/ Safety	After pacer insertion: Roll to <u>left</u> side only or on back ⟶			⟶	
	Bedrest/flat for _____ hours		Ambulate		
	Siderails x _____	Siderails x _____	Siderails x _____		
Diet					

q = every
BID = twice a day
ADL = activities of daily living

FIGURE 5-3 (CONTINUED)
CRITICAL PATH WITH OUTCOME MEASURES

Anticipated Recovery Plan (cont)

Case Type PACEMAKER INSERTION

	Day ___ADM___ Date _____	Day ___1___ Date _____	Day ___2___ Date _____	Day _____ Date _____	Day _____ Date _____
Elimination					
DC Plan	Initiate ARP and review with patient/family Notify Social Service for DC planning	Document and update variances ⟶ Social Service to follow ⟶ Involve family in home plans ⟶ Columbia Park, Brooklyn Center, Fridley Plaza patients enrolled in Pacemaker Checking Program: 1-800-555-5555			
Cardiac Teaching	Notify cardiac educator - Viewed Permanent Pacemaker Video - Given "Living With Your Pacemaker" pamphlet	Reinforce teaching ⟶			
Teaching/ Psychosocial Support	Initiate bedside ARP_____ Instruct to call nurse if chest pain or SOB ⟶ Encourage patient/significant other to ask questions/verbalize concerns ⟶	Review bedside ARP_____ Patient/significant other receive pacemaker pamphlet provided by Pacer Company Instruct patient/significant other in radial pulse taking Review home meds with patient/significant other	Review bedside ARP_____ Reinforce teaching Written & verbal instructions to patient/ significant other to include: - Medications - Diet - Activity guidelines - Wound care - Pacemaker instructions (preprinted) - Community resources - Individualized med card	- Follow-up appointments - Pulse teaching - Troms telephone monitoring - Temporary pacer ID card	
Radiology/ other*	EKG CXR	EKG wtth magnets			
Laboratory*	Lytes, CBC, PT				

ARP = anticipated recovery plan
EKG = electrocardiogram
CBC = complete blood count

FIGURE 5-4
PATIENT CARE MAP

Date/Sign	Patient's Problems	Discharge Outcomes	Intermediate Goals Date Day 1	Date Day 2	Date Day 3	Date Day 4	Date Day 5
1	Impaired mobility	Ambulates independen-ly with assistive device (Specify: walker, _____)		Assists nurse in turning side to side	ROM unaffect-ed extremity	OOB-> Chair with assistance ——→	
	Outcome met (date/sign)						
2	Pain	Pain relieved with oral analgesic	Requests pain med as needed		Pain controlled with PCA or IM med q 3–4 hrs		Pain relieved with IM narcotics q 4–6 hrs
	Outcome met (date/sign)						
3	Potential Complications R/T Immobility a) DVT b) Skin breakdown c) Constipation d) Pneumonia e) Wound infection	a) Without S&S of DVT b) Skin remains intact c) Normal bowel pattern BM q_____ days d) Lungs clear; RR 12–20/min e) Afebrile; incision with-out redness, tenderness, swelling	Maintains fluid/ nutritional intake T, C, DB q 2 hr WA ——→ Uses IS q 1 hr WA ——→			Intake > 1500 cc/day	Maintains/increase weight to baseline ——→ Lists S&S of infec-tion: fever, pain, →drainage
	Outcome met (date/sign)						
4	Potential Bleeding R/T Anticoag Rx	Hemorrhage prevented through early recogni-tion of S&S of bleeding				Lists S&S to report: Palpitations SOB Evidence of blood Variations in pain	
	Outcome met (date/sign)						
5	Self-Care Deficit a) Bathing b) Toileting	a) Performs ADLs with assistance b) Toilets independently				Performs ADLs with assistance Requests help as needed	Uses commode at bedside
	Outcome met (date/sign)					Verbalizes con-cerns to RN ——→	
6	Anxiety	Verbalizes anxiety Participates in care	Identifies plan of care/ expected hos-pital course after instruction				
	Outcome met (date/sign)						

Figure 5-4. This figure shows a sample care map index for a fractured-hip patient. It describes patient outcomes that are scheduled to be achieved based on the interventions listed on the critical path for each day the patient is in the hospital. Whenever a patient does not progress as anticipated, the variance is recorded in the indicated sec-tion of the critical path so all caregivers are quickly aware of the variance and progress can be monitored.

Source: Wood RG, Bailey NO, Tilkemeier D: Managed care: The missing link in quality improvement. *Journal of Nursing Care Quality* 6(4): 58–59, 1992. © 1990. Used with permission of authors and Aspen Publishers, Inc.

FIGURE 5-4 (CONTINUED)
PATIENT CARE MAP

Variance	Date	Day	Date	Day	Date	Day	Date	Day	Date	Day
*Patient										
action taken outcome										
System										
action taken outcome										
Clinician										
action taken outcome										

*Must be documented in nursing progress notes

FIGURE 5-5
ALGORITHM/PATHWAY:
MANAGEMENT OF DVT

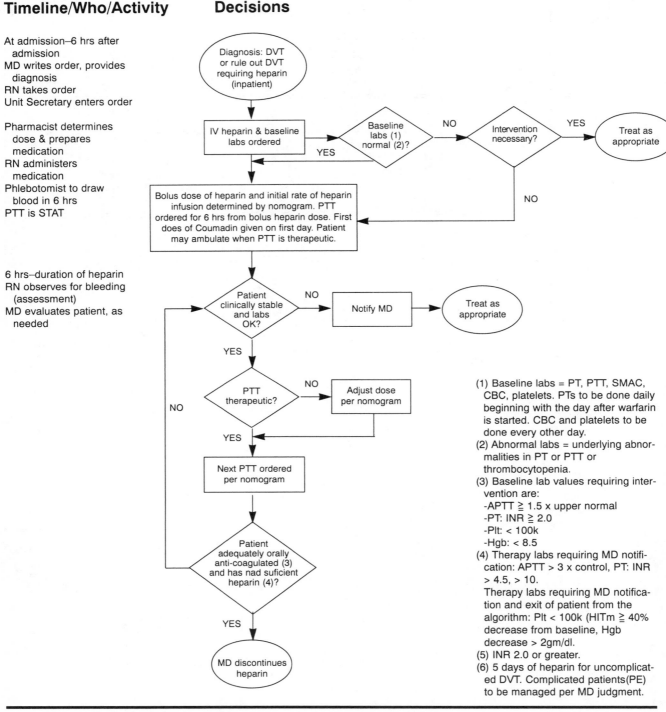

Figure 5-5. This figure shows how a flowchart can be used to document a clinical algorithm, which is used to help reduce variation in a process. The right side reflects the physician decision-making process (clinical algorithm) and is developed by a physician consensus panel and review of the medical literature. The left side reflects actions necessary to carry out these decisions, a timeline of activities, and the personnel involved.

Source: Lutheran General HealthSystem, Park Ridge, IL, 1994. Used with permission.

DATA-COLLECTION TOOLS

This section includes a tool for planning data collection, along with tools to collect indicator data, assess patient/client health status, and report adverse drug reactions.

FIGURE 6-1 (A)
DEVELOPING A DATA-COLLECTION PLAN FOR PERFORMANCE INDICATORS: FLOWCHART

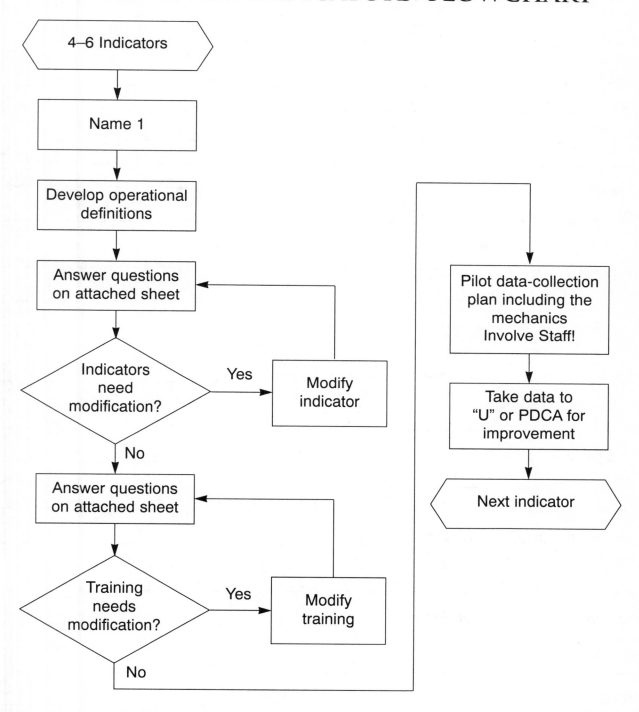

Figure 6-1. This flowchart and worksheet show a process to create a data-collection method for a set of indicators. The flowchart, 6-1(A), identifies the key steps: developing operational definitions, determining how and by whom data are collected, and testing the data-collection plan. The worksheet, 6-1(B), asks key questions about the data-collection plan.

Source: West Paces Medical Center, Atlanta, GA, 1993. Used with permission.

FIGURE 6-1 (B)
DEVELOPING A DATA-COLLECTION PLAN FOR PERFORMANCE INDICATORS: WORKSHEET

DATA-COLLECTION PLAN

Department _____ Process_____

Date _____

Why? _____

_____

_____

What data will be collected? _____

_____

_____

When will the data be collected? _____

_____

_____

How long will the data be collected before initial analysis? _____

_____

_____

Who will collect the data? _____

_____

_____

How will the data be collected? _____

_____

_____

How will the data be analyzed? _____

_____

_____

What training is needed and how will it be accomplished? _____

_____

_____

FIGURE 6-2
SAMPLE CHECKSHEET

Type of Problem	Date and Count of Occurrences					
	10/12	10/13	10/14	10/15	10/16	10/17
Long wait for clean bed	̶|̶|̶|̶|	̶|̶|̶|̶| |	̶|̶|̶|̶| ̶|̶|̶|̶|	|||	̶|̶|̶|̶| ̶|̶|̶|̶|	̶|̶|̶|̶| ̶|̶|̶|̶| |
Waiting for doctor to discharge patients	||	|||	|||	|		|
Transporter not available	||	|	|			||
Not enough admitting clerks	|					
Nurses holding discharges						|
Other	||		|	|		||
Unannounced admit from operating room						

Figure 6-2. This figure shows a common data-collection tool: a checksheet. On the left, columns identify the indicators for which data should be collected. Spaces across the matrix provide space to record each occurrence. This type of form can be used by individual data collectors and can also be used to aggregate data.

FIGURE 6-3
MANUAL DATA-COLLECTION FORM

Medication Use Indicator: "Inpatients Receiving Parenteral Aminoglycosides Who Have a Measured Aminoglycoside Serum Level"*

Medication Use—Form A: Section 1—Data Elements

Complete the following information for the selected patient.

Note: It is necessary that you provide the information below.

Medical Record Number
☐☐☐☐☐☐☐☐☐☐☐☐☐☐☐☐☐☐☐☐

Sample Date:	Admission Date:	Discharge Date:
MM DD YY	MM DD YY	MM DD YY
☐☐/☐☐/☐☐	☐☐/☐☐/☐☐	☐☐/☐☐/☐☐

1. Patient's First Name: ☐☐☐☐☐☐☐☐☐☐☐☐☐☐☐☐☐☐
2. Patient's Last Name: ☐☐☐☐☐☐☐☐☐☐☐☐☐☐☐☐

Indicate whether the patient was receiving one or more of the following three aminoglycosides: Tobramycin, Gentamicin, and/or Amikacin. Excluding Streptomycin, Neomycin, and Paramycin.

3. Is the Patient Receiving an Aminoglycoside?

☐ 1=Yes ⟶ | After completing this section, also complete Section 2. |
☐ 2=No

Indicate whether the patient is receiving one or more of the following medications.

4. Is the Patient Receiving Digoxin? (excluding digitoxin derivatives)

☐ 1=Yes ⟶ | After completing this section, also complete Section 3. |
☐ 2=No

5. Is Patient Receiving Theophylline? (excluding all theophylline derivatives; see definition of terms for a comprehensive list)

☐ 1=Yes ⟶ | After completing this section, also complete Section 3. |
☐ 2=No

---

*This indicator was developed by the Joint Commission Medication Use Indicator Development Task Force.

Figure 6-3. This is an example of a form with which staff can manually collect all the necessary data regarding a specific indicator.

Source: Joint Commission on Accreditation of Healthcare Organizations: *The Measurement Mandate: On the Road to Performance Improvement in Health Care.* Oakbrook Terrace, IL, 1993, pp 152–153.

FIGURE 6-3 (CONTINUED)
MANUAL DATA-COLLECTION FORM

Medication Use Indicator: "Inpatients Receiving Parenteral Aminoglycosides Who Have a Measured Aminoglycoside Serum Level"

Medication Use—Form A: Section 2—Data Elements

Complete the following information for patients who received an aminoglycoside.

Note: It is necessary that you provide the information below.

Medical Record Number

□□□□□□□□□□□□□□□□□□□□

1. Patient's First Name: □□□□□□□□□□□□□□□□□□□□□□

2. Patient's Last Name: □□□□□□□□□□□□□□□□□□□□□

Admission Date: Discharge Date:
MM   DD   YY   MM   DD   YY
□□ / □□ / □□   □□ / □□ / □□

11. Was Aminoglycoside Given Prophylactically?
    □ 1=Yes
    □ 2=No

12. Was a Serum Aminoglycoside Level Drawn?
    □ 1=Yes
    □ 2=No

FIGURE 6-4
INDICATORS FOR CARDIOVASCULAR SERVICES

Cardiac Surgery and Quality Management System

Patient _____

Kaiser # _____

St Vincent # _____

Birth Date _____ Sex _____

Weight_____lbs Height_____in

Admitted _____

Diagnoses _____

_____

Discharge Date _____

Diagnoses _____

_____

Cardiologist _____

Physician _____

Procedure Date _____ Severity _____

Cardiac Surgeon _____

Assistant   #1_____   #2_____   #3_____

Discharge to:

❑ 1 Home   ❑ 3 Kaiser Sunnyside   ❑ 5 Expired
❑ 2 Bess Kaiser   ❑ 4 Nursing Home   ❑ 6 Other (see narrative)

Left Ventricular Function:

❑ 1 Normal (EF > 50%)   ❑ 3 Moderate (EF 31–40%) ❑ 5 not available
❑ 2 Mild (EF 41–50%)   ❑ 4 Severe (EF 0–30%)

Risk Factors:

❑ 1 Diabetic   ❑ 4 Obesity   ❑ 7 Family history
❑ 2 Smoker   ❑ 5 Ex-Smoker   ❑ 8 High cholesterol
❑ 3 Hypertensive   ❑ 6 Previous open heart   ❑ 9 Other (see narrative)

Diabetes: (post-op)   _____Average blood sugar

❑ 1 IV insulin   ❑ 2 Sub-Q insulin

Quality of Service Indicators:

❑ 1 Family reports no surgeon visit   ❑ 4 Transfer summary incomplete
❑ 2 No surgeon visit to patient post-op   ❑ 5 Transfer summary not sent with patient
❑ 3 Cardiologist reports no surgeon call for post-op complication

Blood Products Given:

Reason _____

_____

Figure 6-4. This data collection form pertains to cardiovascular services indicators.

Source: Kaiser Permanente program a prototype for networks? *QI/TQM* 3(9): 130, 1993. Used with permission of Kaiser Permanente Medical Care Program, Northwest Region (Regional Quality Resource Management Department; Portland, OR).

FIGURE 6-4 (CONTINUED)
INDICATORS FOR CARDIOVASCULAR SERVICES

Primary Procedures—Cardiac Surgeon:

❏ 1 Aortic aneurysmectomy
❏ 2 Aortic valve repair
❏ 3 Aortic valve replacement
❏ 4 Coronary artery bypass graft (CABG) w/SVG
❏ 5 CABG w/LV aneurysm resection
❏ 6 CABG w/carotid endarterectomy
❏ 7 CABG w/left internal mammary artery
❏ 8 Congenital disease/defect repair

❏ 9 Mitral valve commissurotomy
❏ 10 Mitral valve repair for mitral regurgitation
❏ 11 Mitral valve replacement
❏ 15 Tricuspid valve repair
❏ 16 Tricuspid valve replacement
❏ 17 Atrial septal defect repair
❏ 18 Ventricular septal defect repair
❏ 99 Other (see narrative)

Non-primary Procedures—Other Surgeon:

❏ 12 Sternal wound repair
❏ 13 Percutaneous transluminal coronary angioplasty (PTCA)

❏ 14 Pericardial surgery
❏ 99 Other (see narrative)

Occurrences:

❏ 1 Intra-aortic balloon pump
❏ 2 Cardiac arrest
❏ 3 Death attributed to surgery within 30 days
❏ 4 Delay in surgery
❏ 5 Documentation inadequate
❏ 6 Deep sternal infection
❏ 7 Peri-op myocardial infarction
❏ 8 Post-op cerebral vascular accident
❏ 9 Post-op transient ischemic attack
❏ 10 Post-op hand weakness/ulnar neuropathy
❏ 11 Post-op hemorrhage
❏ 12 Post-op incisional dehiscence
❏ 13 Post-op incisional hernia
❏ 14 Post-op neurological complication (other)
❏ 15 Post-op renal failure
❏ 16 Post-op thromboembolic event (including deep vein thrombosis and pulmonary embolism)
❏ 17 PTCA as a secondary procedure
❏ 18 Readmit within 31 days related to cardiac surgery
❏ 19 Return to surgery
❏ 20 Transfusion reaction
❏ 21 Unplanned removal/puncture of organ/vessel
❏ 22 Drug toxicity
❏ 23 Post-op dialysis
❏ 24 Re-op within 2 years
❏ 25 Dictated op report not sent w/patient on transfer
❏ 26 Other infection (not deep sternal)
❏ 99 Other (see narrative)

Narrative _____
_____
_____
_____
_____
_____

Reviewer _____ Date _____

FIGURE 6-5
ADMISSION PROCESS SURVEY FORM

Admitting service _____

Type of Bed: _____ICU _____Monitored _____Isolation _____Floor

____ Time admit slip submitted (physician/clerk)
____ Time entered into computer (clerk)
____ Time bed is assigned (clerk)
____ Time bed is ready (clerk)
____ Time patient leaves emergency department (nurse/physician)

Problems
____ No beds in hospital
____ Bed not clean
____ Admitting not aware of bed request
____ Bed not empty yet; no other bed available
____ Bed not empty yet; other empty beds available
____ Nurses in report
____ Bed assigned, but emergency department not notified
____ Service-specified bed not available
____ Other, explain _____

Figure 6-5. This form contains various questions and potential problems related to the admission process. This type of form can be used to collect data as part of an intensive measurement of this process.

Source: Joint Commission on Accreditation of Healthcare Organizations: *The Measurement Mandate: On the Road to Performance Improvement in Health Care* Oakbrook Terrace, IL, 1993, p 177.

FIGURE 6-6
DATA-COLLECTION WORKSHEET

Column	A Wristband absent	B Wristband from another patient	C Patient wearing more than one wristband	D Partially missing ID information	E Partially erroneous ID	F Illegible ID information

Section One:
Patient with Wristband ID Errors

	Patient Name	ID Number	Date	A	B	C	D	E	F
1									
2									
3									
4									
5									
6									
7									
8									

Item G: Total number of patients with ID errors   Totals:

A	B	C	D	E	F

Sample Input Form

Data from Worksheet

1. Total number of errors involving missing wristbands from column A.
2. Total number of errors involving patients wearing another patient's wristband from column B.
3. Total number of errors involving patients wearing more than one different wristband from column C.
4. Total number of errors involving patients wearing wristbands with partially missing information from column D.
5. Total number of errors involving patients wearing wristbands with partially erroneous information from column E.
6. Total number of errors involving patients wearing illegible wristbands from column F.
7. Total number of patients with wristband errors from item G from all worksheets.

Figure 6-6. This tool helps staff collect and aggregate data for specific indicators—in this case, related to wristband ID errors.

Source: Renner SW, Howanitz PJ: Wristband error reporting. 91-01A. In *Q-Probes*. Northfield, IL: College of American Pathologists, 1991. Used with permission.

FIGURE 6-7
EMERGENCY C-SECTION CRITERIA

Physician _____   Patient _____

Time of Decision _____   Time of Incision _____

	Yes	No
A. Fetal Stress		
1. Persistent, severe, variable decelerations		
2. Persistent and non-remediable late decelerations		
3. Persistent, severe bradycardia < 100 BPM		
4. Persistent tachycardia > 180 BPM lasting >10 minutes with decreased variability		
5. Scalp pH <7.2		
6. Prolapsed cord		
B. Maternal Stress		
1. Placenta previa with hemorrhage		
Systolic BP decreased		
30mm Hg from baseline		
Diastolic BP decreased		
15mm Hg from baseline		
Pulse ↑ rapid and thready		
Tachypnea with dyspnea		
2. Abruptio placenta with hemorrhage		
Back pain		
Uterine tenderness		
Rapid uterine contractions; persistent uterine hypertonia		
3. Pregnancy-induced hypertension or severe pre-eclampsia; persistent ↑ BP > 30mm Hg systolic		
Persistent ↑ BP > 15mm Hg diastolic		
↑ BP not resolved with treatment		
Failed induction		
Proteinuria		
Oliguria < 30 cc/hr		
Visual disturbances		
Edema		
Epigastric/URQ pain		
Impaired liver function		
Thrombocytopenia		
If any "yes" answers, was C-section completed within 30 minutes?		
If any "no" answers, was C-section completed within 30 minutes?		
Rationale for C-section not completed within 30 minutes:		

BPM = beats per minute; BP = blood pressure; Hg = mercury

Figure 6-7. This tool is used to review the clinical necessity of an emergency C-section and to determine whether it is completed within the 30-minute standard set by the American College of Obstetricians and Gynecologists.

Source: Improving the timeliness of emergency C-sections at Southwestern Vermont Medical Center leads to improved patient care and increased physician satisfaction. *The Quality Letter for Healthcare Leaders*, Feb 1993, p 8, published by Bader & Associates, Inc. Used with permission.

FIGURE 6-8
SAMPLE DATA-COLLECTION FORM:
FLUOROQUINOLONE USE

Fluoroquinolone Drug Use Evaluation
November 1989

Room #_____

Sex: M   F   Admit Date:_____   Discharge Date:_____
Weight: lbs   kg   Reason for Hospitalization_____
Ciprofloxacin 250   500   750   every 8   12   hours Start: _____
Norfloxacin   400 mg every 12 hours   Stop: _____
Prescribing Physician: _____
                       (if teaching, resident/attending)

Criteria

1. Patient is < 18 years, pregnant or lactating   Yes   No
2. Type of therapy: Prophylactic   Empiric   Precise
      If therapy is PRECISE, Organism: _____
3. Site of infection: Urine   Lung   Bone   Skin   Sinus   Blood
      Other, please specify: _____
4. Antibiotic therapy before fluoroquinolone?   Yes   No   Inpatient   Outpatient
      If YES, please specify drug(s), regimen(s) and start date(s): _____
      _____
      _____

5. Antacids used concurrently? Yes   No   Scheduled administration?   Yes   No
      Ciprofloxacin or norfloxacin administered 2 hr before or 3 hr after antacid?   Yes   No
      If NO, please document resolution of problem on back.
6. Theophylline: Is the patient receiving theophylline?   Yes   No
            If YES: Theophylline level before ciprofloxacin: _____(Mark ND if not done)
                 Theophylline level during ciprofloxacin: _____drawn on _____
                 Was the dose of theophylline changed during ciprofloxacin therapy? Yes   No
                    If YES, what was the new dose _____ mg q _____
                 Did the patient experience theophylline toxicity?   Yes   No
                    If YES, please notify Jayne STAT
7. Patient Outcome: Patient afebrile?   Yes   No   WBC > 2 and < 10   Yes
                 Patient discharged?   Yes   No   WBD differential normal?   Yes
                 Culture at end of treatment?   Yes   No
                 If patient WAS recultured, what were the results?
                                  New organism   Same organism   Negative
                 If the ORGANISM IS NEW, please specify: _____

Laboratory

Date	Serum Creatinine	SGOT	SGPT	LDH	GGPT
_____	_____	_____	_____	_____	_____

Figure 6-8. This is a sample form for collecting data on drug usage. The structure of the form helps ensure all pertinent information is recorded.

Source: Gayman J, Tapley DJ: Drug-usage evaluation and the patient-care pharmacist: A synergistic combination. *Topics in Hospital Pharmacy Management* 11(2): 39, 1991. Used with permission of Aspen Publishers, Inc.

FIGURE 6-9
COLLABORATIVE DATA-COLLECTION TOOL

Date of 7 North Admission: _____

Primary Nurse: _____

Attending MD: _____

Diagnosis: _____

Date of OR (if applicable): _____

Date of each new occurrence								
Skin breakdown								
Surgical wound infection								
DVT								
PE								
Falls								
Fecal impaction								
IV phlebitis								
Pain control								
PCA side effects								
Pneumonia								
Postoperative vomiting								
Other								

Figure 6-9. The data-collection tool for indicators for one nursing unit emphasizes nurse-physician collaboration. Rather than segregating "nursing" indicators and "physician" indicators, this form lists indicators that clearly affect both disciplines and require input from both disciplines for data collection.

Source: Folcarelli PH, et al: Operationalizing collaborative quality assurance: The 7 Gryzmish experience. *Journal of Nursing Care Quality* 7(3): 13, 1993. Used with permission of Aspen Publishers, Inc.

FIGURE 6-10
POST DISCHARGE FOLLOW-UP ASSESSMENT

ASSESSMENT	PROBLEMS IDENTIFIED	NURSING INTERVENTION TEACHING/COUNSELING REFERRAL
Activities of Daily Living		

1. Do you need assistance:
 	
 Walking   Yes_____ No_____
 	
 Sitting   Yes_____ No_____
 	
 Standing   Yes_____ No_____
 	
 Turning in bed Yes_____ No_____
 	
 2. Are you able to get up and get dressed?
    Yes_____ No_____
 	
 3. Do you need help with dressing and grooming?
    Yes_____ No_____
 	
 Is help available? Yes_____ No_____
 	
 Describe _____
 	
 4. What have you been eating since you got home?
 _____
 	
 Are you having difficulties following diet restrictions? Yes_____ No_____
 	
 5. When did you last have a bowel movement?
 _____
 	
 Any problems?
 	
 6. Are you having any difficulties urinating?
    Yes_____ No_____
 Explain _____		

Medications		
1. Did you get your prescriptions filled? Yes_____ No_____ 2. Are you able to take the medications as they were ordered? Yes_____ No_____ 3. Are you having any problems taking your medications? Yes_____ No_____ 4. Are you having any side effects from your medications? Yes_____ No_____		
Symptom Status		
1. Are you having any pain/discomfort? Yes_____ No_____ Where? (location) _____ 2. Are you having other symptoms? Describe: a: _____ b: _____		

Figure 6-10. This form helps nurses collect and assess data about a patient's condition after discharge. Nurses can administer the assessment over the telephone. Based on the assessment, additional teaching, counseling, or referral may be provided.

Source: Phillips CY: Postdischarge follow-up care: Effect on patient outcomes. *Journal of Nursing Care Quality* 7(4): 67–68, 1993. Used with permission of Aspen Publishers, Inc.

FIGURE 6-10 (CONTINUED)
POST DISCHARGE FOLLOW-UP ASSESSMENT

ASSESSMENT	PROBLEMS IDENTIFIED	NURSING INTERVENTION TEACHING/COUNSELING REFERRAL
Surgery Patients		

1. Do you need to change your dressing?
   Yes_____ No_____

   If so, were you adequately taught?
   Yes_____ No_____

   Do you have the equipment and
   supplies you need?   Yes_____ No_____

   Are you managing all right? Yes_____ No_____

   Describe: _____

2. Is your incision red?   Yes_____ No_____

3. Is there drainage from your incision?
   Yes_____ No_____

   If yes, is this drainage pus? Yes_____ No_____

   What color is the drainage? _____

   Amount of drainage? _____

4. Is your incision swollen?   Yes_____ No_____

5. Do you have a fever?   Yes_____ No_____

Agency Referrals	Has been contacted by agency	Has not been contacted by agency	Refused referral
1.			
2.			
3.			
4.			
5.			

Personalized Instructions	States instruction	Does not state instruction	Problems
1. Appointment made with doctor			
2.			
3.			
4.			
5.			

Any other problem or questions you may have: _____

Nursing Assessment

Problems requiring additional nursing assistance

Problem	Recommended follow-up
_____	_____
_____	_____
_____	_____

Functional status of patient/family

_____ Patient/family functioning adequately

_____ Patient/family requires assitance of home nursing care

_____ Patient/family requires assitance of social services

_____ Patient/family requires medical assessment at this time

_____ Patient/family requires other referral (please specify) _____

Nurse Signature_____   Time Spent in Interview _____ _____min

FIGURE 6-11
PATIENT STATUS SELF-ASSESSMENT

OSTEOARTHRITIS OF THE KNEE Form 16.1   Date: ____ Mo ____ Day ____ Yr

Instructions:

This survey asks for your views about the way your arthritis affects your health. This information will be summarizied in your medical record and will help your doctors keep track of how you feel. Answer every question by circling the appropriate number, 1, 2, 3... If you are unsure about how to answer a question, please give the best answer you can and make a comment in the left margin.

1. Who completed this form? (circle one number)

I filled it out with no help	1
I filled it out with help of family and friends	2
I filled it out with help from a healthcare provider	3
Family or friends	4
Healthcare provider	5

Mode of Collection

Self-administered	1 ☐
Personal interview	2 ☐
Telephone interview	3 ☐
Mail	4 ☐
Other	5 ☐

Functional Status Assessment (circle Yes/No for each item)

2. When you travel around the community, does someone have to assist you <u>because of your knee arthritis</u>?
        YES   NO

3. Are you in bed or in a chair for most or all of the day <u>because of your knee arthritis</u>?
        YES   NO

4. Do you have trouble either walking <u>several</u> blocks or climbing a <u>few</u> flights of stairs <u>because of your knee arthritis</u>?
        YES   NO

5. Do you have any trouble either walking <u>one</u> block or climbing <u>one</u> flight of stairs <u>because of your knee arthritis</u>?
        YES   NO

Circle one number for each question below.

6. During the <u>past month</u>, how would you describe the <u>knee pain</u> you usually have?

very severe	severe	mild	very mild	none
1	2	3	4	5

7. During the <u>past month</u>, how often have you had severe <u>knee pain</u> from your arthritis?

always	very often	fairly often	sometimes	almost never	never
1	2	3	4	5	6

8. During the <u>past month</u>, how often has your <u>knee pain</u> interfered with your sleeping?

always	very often	fairly often	sometimes	almost never	never
1	2	3	4	5	6

9. During the <u>past month</u>, how often have you had to take medication for your <u>knee arthritis</u>?

every day	most days	half the days	some days	few days	never
1	2	3	4	5	6

10. How often do you have to use a walking aid (such as a cane, crutches, or walker) because of your <u>knee arthritis</u>?

every day	most days	half the days	some days	few days	never
1	2	3	4	5	6

11. During the <u>past month</u>, how active has your <u>knee arthritis</u> been?

very active	moderately active	mildly active	not at all active
1	2	3	4

12. Considering the way that your <u>knee arthritis</u> affects you, how well are you doing?

very well	well	fair	poor	very poor
1	2	3	4	5

Figure 6-11. This tool longitudinally measures patients' health status. Patients complete the questionnaire during initial and follow-up visits.

Source: Patients' evaluation of their health status. *The Quality Letter for Healthcare Leaders*, Mar 1992, p 22. Form © The Health Outcomes Institute, Bloomington, MN. All rights reserved. Used with permission.

FIGURE 6-12
PATIENT STATUS ASSESSMENT

OSTEOARTHRITIS OF THE KNEE   Date: ____Mo ____Day ____Yr
Form 16.2

Clinical Data and Physical Exam
1. Diagnosis*—Osteoarthritis of the knee on x-ray

	Right	**Left**
Medial compartment	_____	_____
Lateral compartment	_____	_____

[Kellgram & Lawrence criteria—grade each from 0 to 4 where 0=no change, 1=minimal change, 2=osteophytes, 3=joint space narrowing, 4=severe joint space narrowing; any singe grade of 2 is a diagnosis of osteoarthritis.]

	Right	**Left**
2. Disease severity score *(total score from x-ray grades)*	_____	_____

3. Joint tenderness on direct palpitation

	Right	**Left**
Medial joint line tenderness	_____	_____
Lateral joint line tenderness	_____	_____
Summary score	_____	_____

[Score: 0=no tenderness, 1=tenderness only when you ask patient, 2=patient volunteers response, 3=patient winces and withdraws; summary score is combined score for the right and left.]

4. Instability

	Right	**Left**
Medial ligament	_____	_____
Lateral ligament	_____	_____

[Score: 0=none (0°–5°), 1=slight (5°–10°), 2=definite (10°–20°), 3=severe instability (> 20°)] (range 0°–7° for the left and right)]

5. Range of motion in degrees (normal=0°–150°)

	Right	**Left**
Flexion	_____	_____
Extension	_____	_____

6. Disease duration*   _____ Years
*Years since patient has had knee pain for most days of the month.

Figure 6-12. This form reports a patient's functional and clinical status. Completed by the physician, the tool aids the longitudinal measurement of patients' health care.

Source: Patients' evaluation of their health status. *The Quality Letter for Healthcare Leaders*, Mar 1992, p 23. Form © The Health Outcomes Institute, Bloomington, MN. All rights reserved. Used with permission.

FIGURE 6-13
DATA-COLLECTION FORM

Pickup date	Floor (unit)	Patient		Admit date	Discharge date	Part (P)/ Chart (C)	Found		Department Data		
		Name	Number				Where	Date	LOS	Transfer	MDs

LOS = length of stay

Figure 6-13. This form is used for providing pertinent information for eliminating possible causes of missing parts of charts. It is designed to allow data collectors to record the required data in a quick and efficient manner.

Source: Hopkins G, Doggett S: Enhancing hospital cash flow through improved medical records processing. *Quality Management in Health Care* 1(2): 28, 1993. Used with permission of Aspen Publishers, Inc.

FIGURE 6-14 (A)
MEDICATION VARIANCE REPORT

Medical record no. ☐☐☐☐☐☐

Date of variance ☐☐☐☐☐☐   Time of variance ☐☐☐☐☐☐   Dept/Unit # ☐☐☐

Inpatient ☐   Male ☐   Medication _____
Outpatient ☐   Female ☐   Patient Diagnosis _____

A. Explain what happened, why it happened, and what was done to minimize its effect on the patient:

_____

_____

B. What was done to prevent this type of incident from recurring?

_____

_____

_____

_____

_____

_____

_____

_____

_____

_____

_____

_____

_____

_____

_____

_____

_____

_____

Signature of preparer _____   Date _____

Supervisor's Signature _____   Date _____

Figure 6-14. This two-part medication error form combines measurement and assessment. The streamlined form is designed to report, track, assess, and correct medication errors, with an emphasis on processes rather than individuals. Part one, 6-14(A), is the data collection and assessment form; part two, 6-14(B), provides instructions for filling out the form.

Source: Hospital uses CQI to attack medication errors, reporting. *QI/TQM*, February 1993, p 24. Used with permission from Athens Regional Medical Center, Athens, GA.

FIGURE 6-14 (B)
MEDICATION VARIANCE REPORT

ARMC Reporting Guidelines are given to provide instructions and a standard procedure for completing the variance. The purpose in reporting a medication variance is to enable personnel to take different steps to avoid similar situations in the future. Remember that giving medications is a process with different steps. Ask yourself what steps were missed?

Stamp patient's blue charge
addressograph

Date of variance: Month, day, and year. When did it happen?
Time of variance: Use military time or indicate AM or PM. What time was the medication given/omitted?
Dept/Unit #: Your area's cost code number.

What was the patient's status?	What was the patient's sex?	Medication: What was ordered? What was given? Patient Diagnosis: What is the physician's current diagnosis of the patient?		
Type of Variance: What kind of variance happened?	Route of Administration: How was the medication given?	Genesis: Origin of the variance. What was the first thing that happened to make things go wrong?	Person Responsible: Who actually gave the medication?	Effect on Patient: What happened to the patient after taking the medication?
				No effect: Nothing happened Minimal effect: Drowsy Moderate effect: Stupor Severe effect: Respiratory apnea/arrest Death...
			The attending physician must always be notified ASAP. Risk management should be notified to ascertain risk. Patient and family awareness of the variance should be found out, but they do not necessarily need to be told. Please note any reaction in detail.	

Please answer all Questions A and B in as much detail as possible. Make sure you address every area.
In conclusion: The person having the most knowledge concerning the variance should complete the written report. Usually the person who gave the medication has the most information, but sometimes it is the discoverer.

This form shall not be used to document "paper errors" or because the patient was NPO, off the unit, and so forth. It shall not include opinions and hearsay.

Please notify these people whenever there is a medication variance:
1) The attending physician
2) The nursing supervisor
3) The head nurse
4) Risk management

Any questions or difficulty filling out this form? Please call the Quality Assurance Department for assistance.

NPO = nothing by mouth

FIGURE 6-15
ADVERSE DRUG REACTION REPORT

Drug Experience Report: Internal Report for P&T Committee Use Only.
To be completed by any health care professional.
An adverse drug reaction is a reaction that is noxious, unintended, unpredictable, and occurs at doses normally used in humans for prophylaxis, diagnosis, or therapy of the disease.

I. Reaction Information

1. Patient ID/Initials (in confidence)	2. Age	3. Sex	4. Wt	5. Ht

6. Reporting Date Mo Day Yr	7. Reaction Onset Date Mo Day Yr	8. Describe Suspected Reactions

9. Outcome of Reaction to Date

❑ Alive with sequelae   ❑ Recovered   ❑ Still under treatment for reaction   ❑ Died (give cause, date)

10. Tests/Laboratory Data Confirming Reaction (include biopsy and/or autopsy results)	11. Was Hospital Treatment for Reaction Required? ❑ Yes ❑ No

II. Suspected Drugs Information

12. Suspect Drug(s) Trade/Generic Name Manufacturer	13. Total Daily Dose
	14. Route of Administration

15. Indication(s) for Use	16. Therapy Dates From To	17. Therapy Duration

18a. Was Treatment with Suspected Drug Reduced in Dosage? Yes No Discontinued	18b. Did Reaction Abate? Yes No	19. Was Drug Reintroduced or Dose Decreased?

20. Did Reaction Disappear?   Yes   No

III. Recent/Concomitant Drugs and Medical Problems

21. Other Drugs	Total Daily Dose	Route	Dates/Duration of Administration	Indication

22. Describe Other Relevant Medical History (for example, allergies, environmental or occupational exposure, previous drug reactions, pregnancy with gravidity, parity, or ethnic origin):

23. Reporter Name (in confidence)

Figure 6-15. This report helps staff inform the pharmacy about adverse drug reactions.

Source: Guharoy SR: A pharmacy-coordinated, multidisciplinary approach for successful implementation of an adverse drug reaction reporting program. *Topics in Hospital Pharmacy Management* 12(2): 70–71, 1992. Used with permission of Sudip Roy Guharoy, PharmD, John F. Kennedy Memorial Hospital, Indio, CA.

FIGURE 6-16
ADVERSE DRUG REACTION REPORT

Patient Initial (optional)	Age (or Date of Birth)	Sex Male Female	Date of Reaction Onset
Medical Record #	Room # or Unit	Service	Date Report Submitted

Describe the Reaction.
   (Please Note: Only reactions meeting at least one of the criteria on the next page should be reported.)

Suspected Drug(s), Dose, Route of Administration, and Duration of Use.

Reason(s) This Is Suspected Cause of the Reaction.

Drugs Taken Concomitantly.
Drug   Dose   Route (PO, IV, IM, and so forth)

Send completed forms to Secretary, Pharmacy & Therapeutics Committee
Box J-316 JHMHC

Submitted by: _____   ❏ MD ❏ RPh ❏ RN ❏ Other _____
                                     (Print)
                                                                Signature: _____

PO=by mouth; IV=intravenous; IM=intramuscular.

Figure 6-16. This sample adverse drug reaction reporting form lists the criteria for reporting adverse reactions, including those that cause a report to be forwarded to the Food and Drug Administration.

Source: Hatton RC: Criteria-based adverse drug reaction reporting and the use of a relational database. *Topics in Hospital Pharmacy Management* 12(2): 42–43, 1992. Used with permission of Shands Hospital at the University of Florida.

FIGURE 6-16 (CONTINUED)
ADVERSE DRUG REACTION REPORT

An Adverse Drug Reaction is defined as any response to a drug that is noxious and unintended and that occurs at doses used in humans for prophylaxis, diagnosis, or therapy, excluding therapeutic failure to accomplish the intended purpose. These reactions are primarily immunologic or idiosyncratic in nature. For educational purposes, adverse drug reactions that are predictable, serious, or prolong hospital stay, and that can be prevented by appropriate dosing and/or administration technique, are reportable. Predictable reactions may be an extension of the drug's pharmacologic and/or toxicologic effect and, therefore, include intentional or accidental drug overdoses.

An Adverse Drug Reaction Report does not indicate that the drug was the cause of the reaction, only that there is suspicion. All reactions detected that meet at least one of the criteria listed below are reportable.

Criteria for Reporting Adverse Drug Reactions (ADR)
(Check all that apply)

* ❑   The patient died.
* ❑   The reaction was permanently disabling.
* ❑   The reaction was life-threatening.
* ❑   The reaction was the cause of hospitalization.
* ❑   The reaction prolonged hospitalization.
* ❑   The reaction is attributed to an investigational drug.
* ❑   The suspected drug causing the reaction has been on the market less than two years.
* ❑   The reaction is not listed in the package insert (or PDR).
* ❑   The reaction is a teratogenic effect.
   ❑   The reaction was the reason for a change in the patient's drug therapy.
   ❑   The reaction required treatment with a drug or other therapy.
   ❑   The reaction was the result of a drug-drug interaction.
   ❑   The reaction was the result of a drug-food interaction.
   ❑   An increased cluster (or frequency) of the reaction is occurring.
   ❑   The adverse reaction is the result of an intentional overdose.
   ❑   The adverse reaction is the result of an iatrogenic overdose.
   ❑   The reaction is the result of a medication error.

*Criteria designated with an asterisk indicate that the ADR report will automatically be forwarded to the Food and Drug Administration. Those without an asterisk will be evaluated on an individual basis.

PDR=Physician's Desk Reference

This report is a Pharmacy and Therapeutics Committee Investigatory Record and is CONFIDENTIAL. Do NOT retain a copy of this report for your records.

DATA-DISPLAY TOOL

This section presents control charts, run charts, and other methods to illustrate performance and thereby help detect trends and patterns.

FIGURE 7-1
SAMPLE CONTROL CHARTS

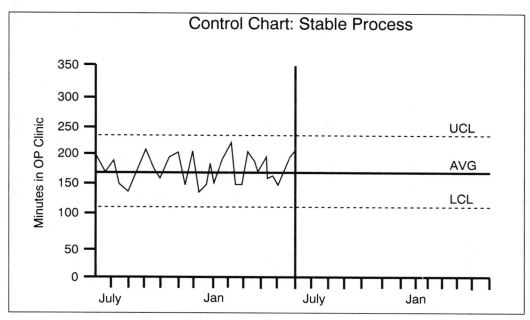

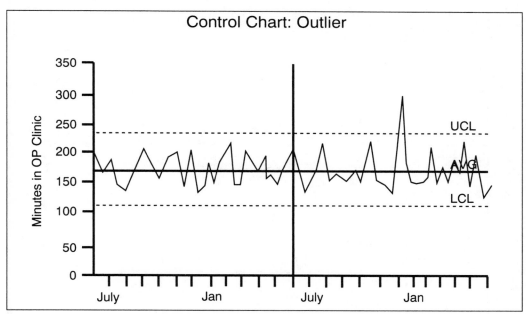

Figure 7-1. This series of five control charts illustrates different patterns of performance an organization is likely to encounter. A control chart is a run chart with statistically determined upper and lower control limits. When performance is within those limits, the process is said to be "in control." In control does not mean desirable; rather, it means the process is stable, not affected by special causes of variation (such as equipment failure). A process must be in control before it can be systematically improved.

The five figures show the following scenarios:

Stable Process. All points are within the control limits. The process is thus stable or in control.

Outlier. One point jumps outside a control limit. Staff should determine whether this single occurrence is likely to recur.

FIGURE 7-1 (CONTINUED)
SAMPLE CONTROL CHARTS

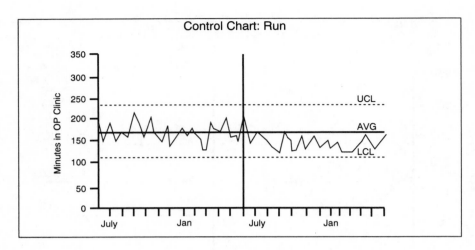

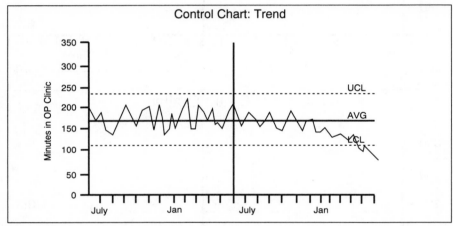

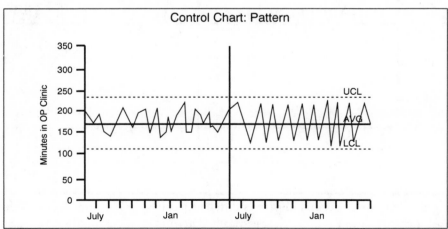

Run. A run occurs when a given number or points in a row are on one or the other side of the average. This may suggest an opportunity for improvement.

Trend. A trend is a steady rise or fall in performance. Trends headed toward or crossing control limits suggest further assessment is necessary.

Pattern. An identifiable pattern in performance such as that shown here may indicate a performance problem associated with factors such as time of day, shift, season, and so forth.

FIGURE 7-2
RATES OF MECHANICAL EXTRACTION

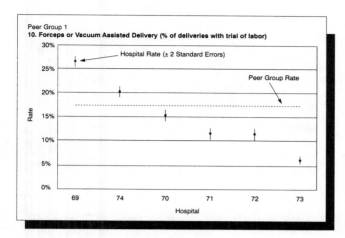

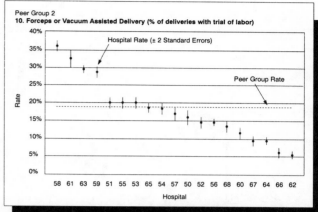

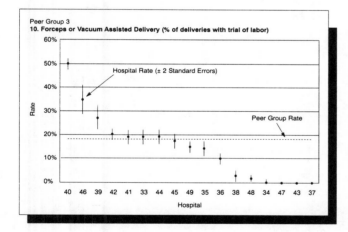

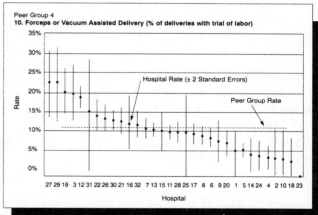

Figure 7-2. These charts display aggregate data related to forceps or vacuum-assisted delivery. These charts are basically run charts with bars representing plus or minus two standard errors. Smaller error bars indicate a higher number of deliveries and a more reliable estimate of the true rates of extraction.

Source: Jones L: StORQS: Washington's statewide obstetrical review and quality system: Overview and provider evaluation. *QRB*, Apr 1993, p 115. © 1993 Joint Commission on Accreditation of Healthcare Organizations.

FIGURE 7-3
PERFORMANCE GOALS AND
ACTUAL PERFORMANCE

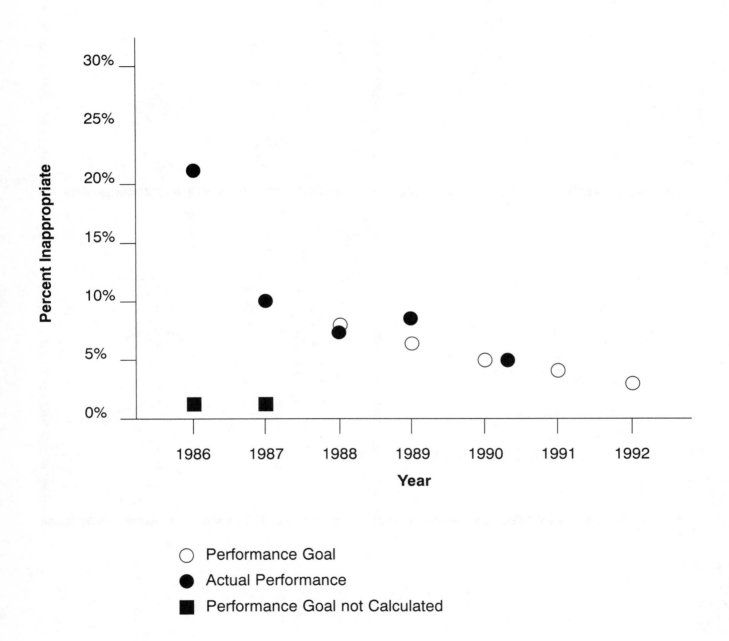

Figure 7-3. This variation on a run chart compares actual performance with performance goals for each year. This example displays the percentages of "inappropriate" in-hospital days.

Source: Payne SMC, et al: New methods for evaluating utilization management programs. *QRB*, Oct 1992, p 347. ©1992 Joint Commission on Accreditation of Healthcare Organizations.

FIGURE 7-4
COMPARATIVE PERFORMANCE: MISSING MEDICATION REQUESTS

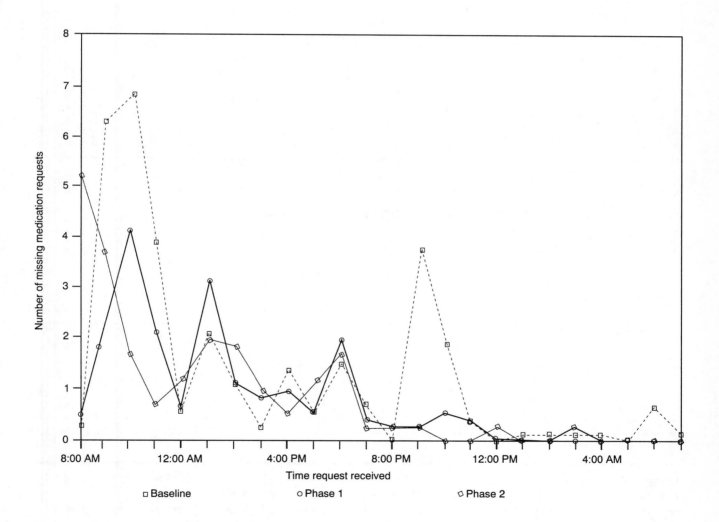

Figure 7-4. This figure superimposes three run charts. One line and set of symbols shows baseline performance, the second shows performance after internal pharmacy-system changes, and the third shows performance after pharmacy-personnel activity changes. This format helps assess results of specific improvement efforts.

Source: Peterson AM, et al: A systems approach to the problem of missing medications. *Topics in Hospital Pharmacy Management* 11(1): 74, 1991. Used with permission of Aspen Publishers, Inc.

FIGURE 7-5
HISTOGRAMS

Illustrations of Variability

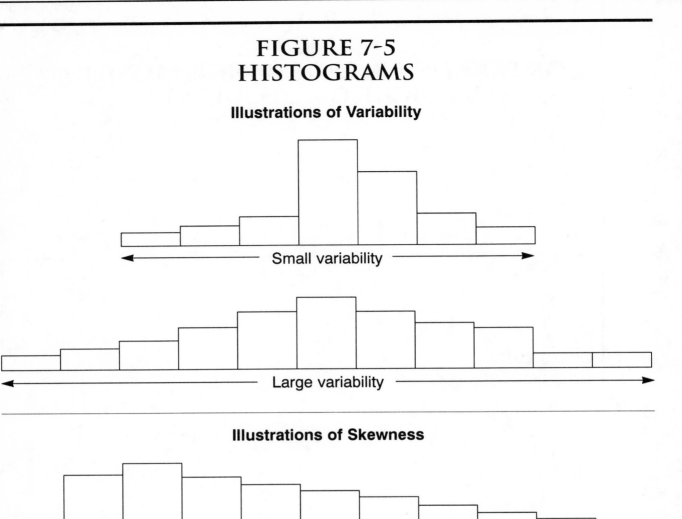

Illustrations of Skewness

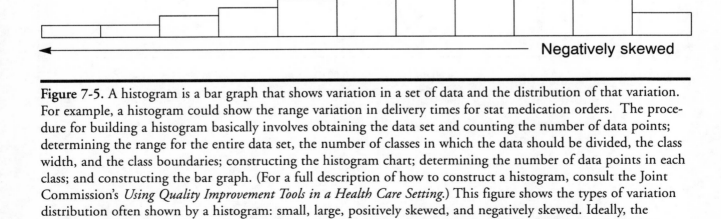

Figure 7-5. A histogram is a bar graph that shows variation in a set of data and the distribution of that variation. For example, a histogram could show the range variation in delivery times for stat medication orders. The procedure for building a histogram basically involves obtaining the data set and counting the number of data points; determining the range for the entire data set, the number of classes in which the data should be divided, the class width, and the class boundaries; constructing the histogram chart; determining the number of data points in each class; and constructing the bar graph. (For a full description of how to construct a histogram, consult the Joint Commission's *Using Quality Improvement Tools in a Health Care Setting.*) This figure shows the types of variation distribution often shown by a histogram: small, large, positively skewed, and negatively skewed. Ideally, the distribution is symmetrical and the variation small. Used with permission from GOAL/QPC, 13 Branch Street, Methuen, MA 01844-1953. Tel: 508/685-3900.

Source: *The Memory Jogger: A Pocket Guide of Tools for Continuous Improvement.* ©1988 GOAL QPC.

CAUSAL-
ANALYSIS
TOOLS

These tools, including cause-and-effect diagrams and Pareto charts, help
determinine the underlying causes of performance conditions or problems and thereby
identify potential areas for improvement.

FIGURE 8-1
CAUSE-AND-EFFECT DIAGRAM:
CODING INCONSISTENCIES

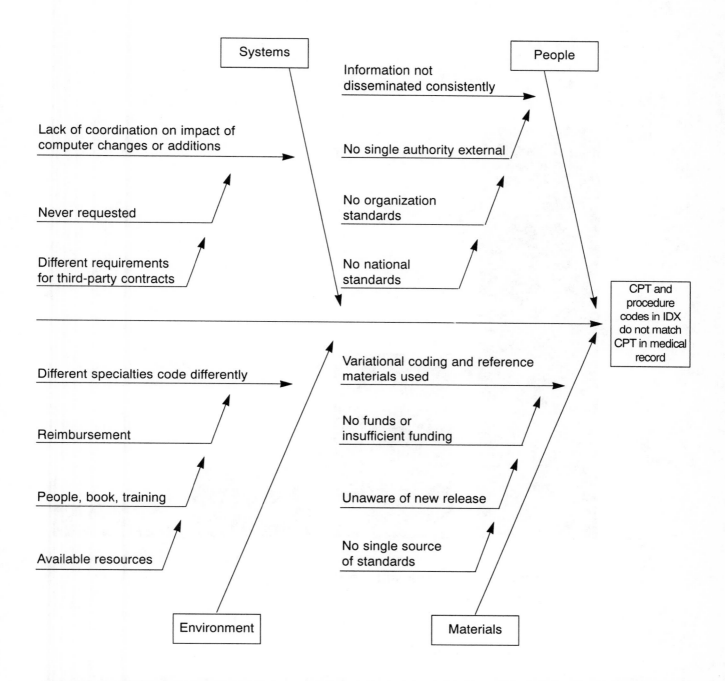

Figure 8-1. A cause-and-effect diagram (also called a fishbone or Ishikawa diagram) is used to gather and organize possible causes of a specific outcome. The larger box on the right contains the outcome. The four smaller boxes contain the factors influencing the outcome. Next to each box is a chain of causes, tracing causality from the root cause to the final effect.

Source: Creps LB, et al: Performance improvement review: Implementation of total quality in medical information services. *Topics in Health Information Management* 14(2): 73, 1993. Used with permission of Aspen Publishers, Inc.

FIGURE 8-2
PARETO CHART

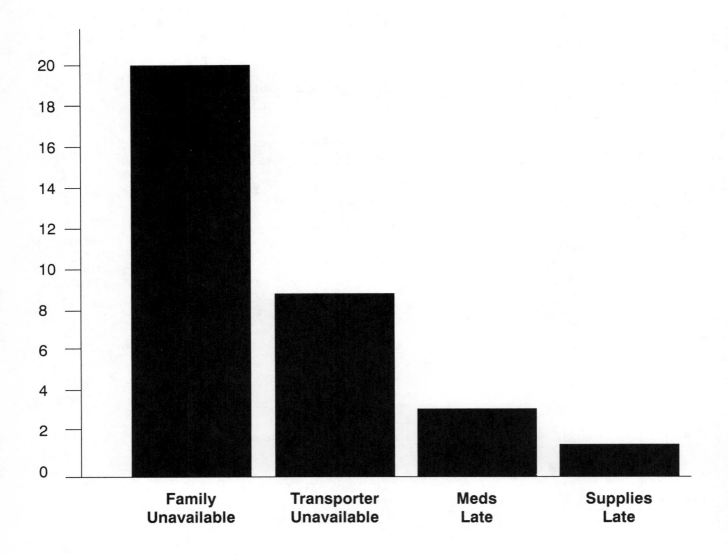

Figure 8-2. A Pareto chart often shows that only one or two causes are responsible for many occurrences. This example reflects that unavailable family and unavailable transporter are responsible for over 82% of delays. A Pareto chart can help staff determine the cause of a performance pattern so improvement actions can be appropriately directed.

FIGURE 8-3
PARETO CHART WITH CUMULATIVE PERCENTAGE

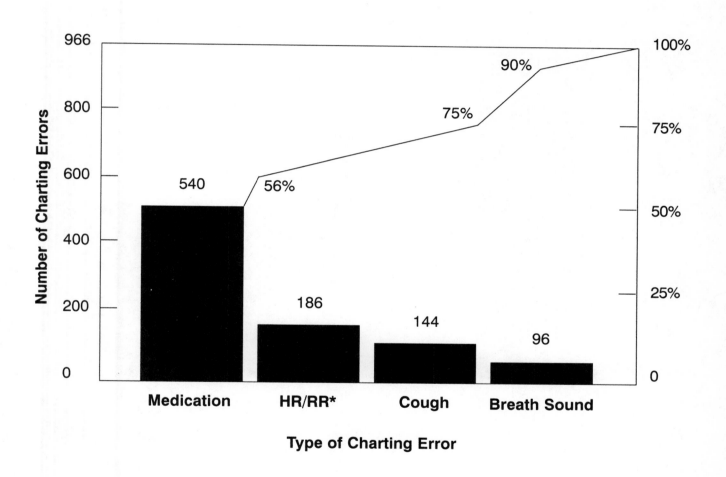

*Denotes heart rate/respiratory rate documentation

Figure 8-3. This Pareto chart is from a respiratory care department and illustrates aerosol treatment charting errors by type of error. This example includes a line showing cumulative percentage.

Source: Klepcyk JC: Total quality management: Defining a process for quality improvement. *Topics in Hospital Pharmacy Management* 12(4): 32, 1993. Used with permission of Aspen Publishers, Inc.

TOOLS FOR SELECTING AND IMPLEMENTING IMPROVEMENTS

These tools can help teams select improvement actions, test those actions, and implement the actions in a systematic way.

FIGURE 9-1
BARRIERS AND AIDS ANALYSIS

Countermeasure	Barriers	Rank	Aids	Rank
Open storeroom	Acceptance by people	H	Decrease wait time	H
	Possible lost paperwork	L	Decrease paperwork	L
	Requires additional training	M	Could reduce staff in storeroom	M
	Possibility for theft	L	Increase productivity	M
	Cost	L	Increase customer satisfaction	M
	Requires trust of customer	M		

Ranking:
H = High
M = Medium
L = Low

Figure 9-1. This figure shows a technique for identifying and analyzing elements that resist change (barriers) or push for change (aids). This analysis encourages the team to be proactive in planning a smooth implementation of the countermeasures and helps ensure a successful project.

Source: Klepcyk JC: Total quality management: Defining a process for quality improvement. *Topics in Hospital Pharmacy Management* 12(4): 37, 1993. Used with permission of Aspen Publishers, Inc.

FIGURE 9-2
COUNTERMEASURES MATRIX

Problem	Root cause	Counter-measures	Practical methods	Effectiveness	Feasibility	Overall	Action
The problem that needs correction	Identified on cause-and-effect diagram and verified	Specifically aimed at the root causes and are within the team's ability to implement A counter-measure is the *what*. The practical method is the *how*.	A specific task needed to accomplish the countermeasures	A rating based on how much the countermeasure will reduce the root cause The higher rating goes to the more effective countermeasure	A rating based on the time, cost, work, and acceptance needed to implement countermeasure The higher rating goes to the more effective countermeasure	The product of effectiveness x feasibility This serves as a ranking of the countermeasures for action	Indicated by YES or NO if action will be taken

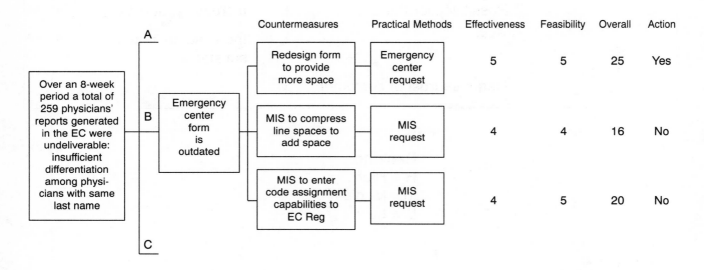

Scale: 1 = None; 2 = Somewhat; 3 = Moderate; 4 = Very; 5 = Extreme

Figure 9-2. A countermeasures matrix helps a team show the relationships between effect, root causes, and countermeasures. As explained in the first part of this figure, the matrix is composed of the following components: the problem being addressed, the problem's root cause, possible countermeasures to address the root cause, practical methods to carry out each countermeasure, the potential effectiveness of the countermeasure, the feasibility of carrying out the countermeasure, the overall ranking of the countermeasure's desirability, and the decision whether to take action by implementing the countermeasures. The second part of this figure shows a countermeasure matrix developed by an emergency center quality improvement team.

Source: Klepcyk JC: Total quality management: Defining a process for quality improvement. *Topics in Hospital Pharmacy Management* 12(4): 35–36, 1993. Used with permission of Aspen Publishers, Inc.

FIGURE 9-3
SAMPLE SELECTION GRID FOR IMPROVEMENT ACTIONS

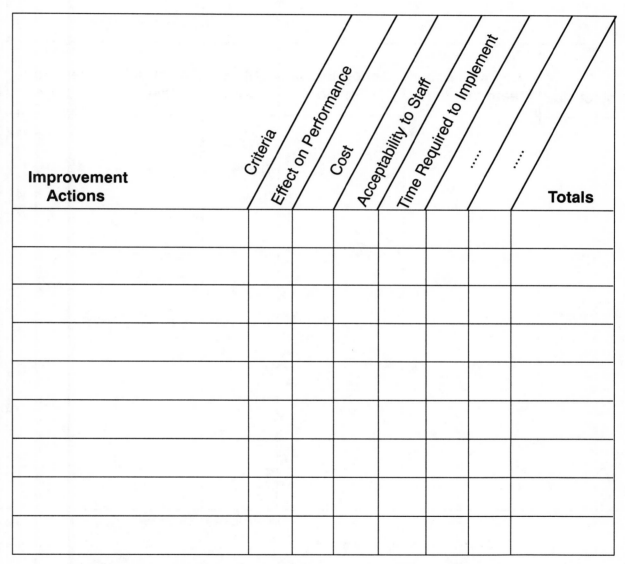

Use 1-5 scale to rate each proposed solution against each criterion.
1 = Most positive impact
5 = Lease positive impact

Figure 9-3. Once a team has identified possible actions to improve performance, it can use this grid to help determine which action is most appropriate. The potential solutions are listed down the left side. Each is assigned a score of 1 to 5 for a specific criterion, such as effect on performance and cost. The totals should show whether one possible improvement action is clearly preferable.

FIGURE 9-4
TRACKING LOG FOR IMPROVEMENT
ACTIONS BEING TESTED

Project No.	Departments/ Team Involved	Action Being Tested	Start Date	Completion Date	Results to Date

Figure 9-4. This sample tracking log can be used to oversee process changes being tested in an organization.

FIGURE 9-5
GANTT CHART: IMPROVING MEDICATION DISTRIBUTION

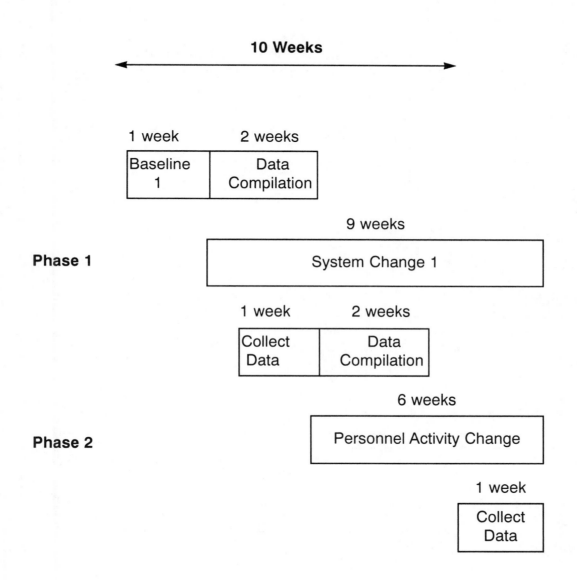

Figure 9-5. This Gantt chart depicts relative implementation time for each phase of a sequential intervention strategy to reduce the number of missing medications.

Source: Peterson AM, et al: A systems approach to the problem of missing medications. *Topics in Hospital Pharmacy Management* 11(1): 72, 1991. Used with permission of Aspen Publishers, Inc.

FIGURE 9-6
PLANNING GRIDS FOR IMPROVEMENT ACTIONS

GOAL:					
Strategies	Expected Results	Resource Requirements	Who's Responsible	Target Date(s)	Actions

GOAL:				
Strategies	Who	When	Additional Results	How to Evaluate

GOAL:				
Strategies	Expected Results	Additional Results	Target Date	Action

Figure 9-6. These three formats can help any group plan and carry out the actions necessary to meet a specific improvement goal. The grids identify various information necessary to oversee improvement activities, including strategies, dates, and responsible parties.

FIGURE 9-7
PROCESS DECISION PROGRAM CHART

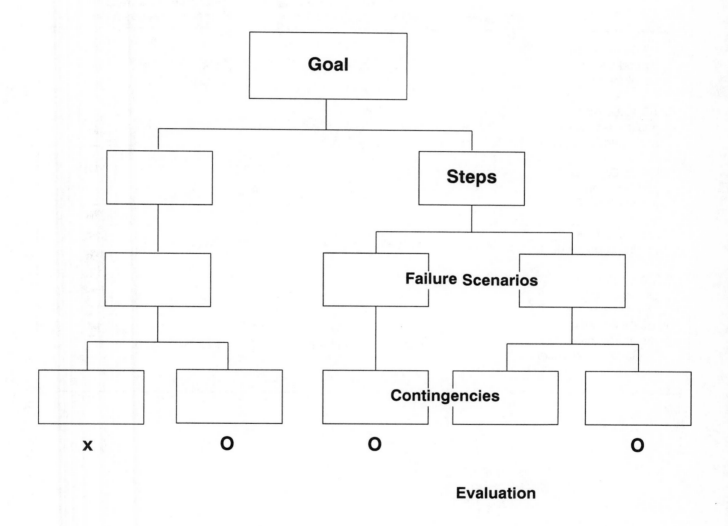

Figure 9-7. This chart maps out conceivable but undesirable events in a plan and indicates appropriate responses. It is usually used near the end of a planning effort as a final check of potential problem-prone elements in the plan. The symbol "X" marks impractical contingencies and the "O" marks those that should be used.

Source: Plsek PE: Tutorial: Management and planning tools of TQM. *Quality Management in Health Care* 1(3): 63, 1993. Used with permission of Aspen Publishers, Inc.

FIGURE 9-8
IMPLEMENTATION WORKPLAN

			Revised Dates and Usage			
Name	**Start**	**End**	**Duration Status** **Business Days**	**Resource Assignments** **Name**	**Usage**	**Cost**
06.03.00 Functional procedure development						
06.03.10.03 M/R design user manual and operations guide	8/6/90	8/20/90	11	L. Paige	14.0	0
06.06.00 Controls, policies, and procedures (CPP)						
06.06.40.03 M/R review control design	8/15/90	8/20/90	4	L. Paige	1.0	0
06.08.00 User training (UT)						
06.08.08.03 M/R UT secure facilities and equipment train users	8/15/90	8/20/90	4	L. Paige	34.0	0

M/R =

Figure 9-8. This form documents a workplan for implementing a new system—in this case, an automated billing system. The form includes selected stages of the plan, assigned completion dates and estimated hours of each stage, responsible individuals, and cost estimates. Such a format could also be used in a redesign effort.

Source: Paige L: Implementing a mainframe coding/abstracting system. *Topics in Health Information Management* 13(1): 29, 1992. Used with permission of Aspen Publishers, Inc.

FIGURE 9-9
IMPLEMENTATION PROJECT TESTING PROBLEM LIST

Status: 1. Being processed by IS (open)
        2. Being processed by   (open)
        3. In testing (open)
        4. Completed
        5. Modification identified

Priority: 1. Necessary for go-live
         2. Post-implementation

SPSR #	Date	Error Description	Resp Party	Status	Priority	Comp. Date	Comp By	Comments
0296.1	10/23/90	Invalid diagnosis code	IS	44	1	10/24/90	IS	
0296.2	10/23/90	Abend on MR abstract	IS	4	1	10/30/90	IS	
0297.0	10/24/90	Incorrect printing of statement of account	IS	1	1			
0297.1	10/24/90	Series error on KP100BC report with batch charges	IS	1	1			
0297.2	10/24/90	Insurance relationship wording not corrected (0242.6)	IS	4	1	10/25/90	IS	
0298.0	10/25/90	Need PAM detail on KP920BC	IS	1	1			
0298.1	10/25/90	Charges did not pass from PCS to Medipac	IS	4	1	11/2/90	IS	
0298.2	09/24/90	Unable to access account by pt acct# in MR abstract	IS	4	1	10/26/90	IS	
0302.0	10/29/90	Discharge date not passing to MR	IS	4	1	10/29/90	IS	
0302.1	10/29/90	Abend on abstract	IS	4	1	10/30/90	IS	
0302.2	10/29/90	Incorrect UB82 revenue codes	FIN	4		10/29/90	FIN	
0302.3	10/29/90	Incorrect UB82 revenue codes	FIN	1	1	10/29/90		
0302.4	10/29/90	Block 57 on UB82 incorrect for Blue Cross	IS	1	1			
0303.0	10/30/90	DRG code not carrying from MR to IAR	IS	1	1			
0304.0	10/30/90	Cannot access patient by acct# or MR# in MR abstract	IS	1	1			
0304.1	10/31/90	No error for 2 patients in same room/bed	IS	1	1			
0305.1	11/1/90	Discharge reversal not working in Medipac	IS	1	1			
0305.2	10/30/90	Dr# not passing to UB82. Problem 0276.12 reoccurring	IS	1	1			
0305.3	11/1/90	Medicaid# not printing on UB82 correctly	IS	1	1			
0307.0	10/30/90	Bill type needs to be 132 on series bill	IS	1	2			

Figure 9-9. Testing is a key part of implementing any new process or system. This is a format for dealing with problems identified when implementing an automated billing system. As problems were identified, they were documented on a problem list for the technical staff.

Source: Paige L: Implementing a mainframe coding/abstracting system. *Topics in Health Information Management* 13(1): 32, 1992. Used with permission of Miami Valley Hospital, Dayton, OH.

FIGURE 9-10
TREE DIAGRAM

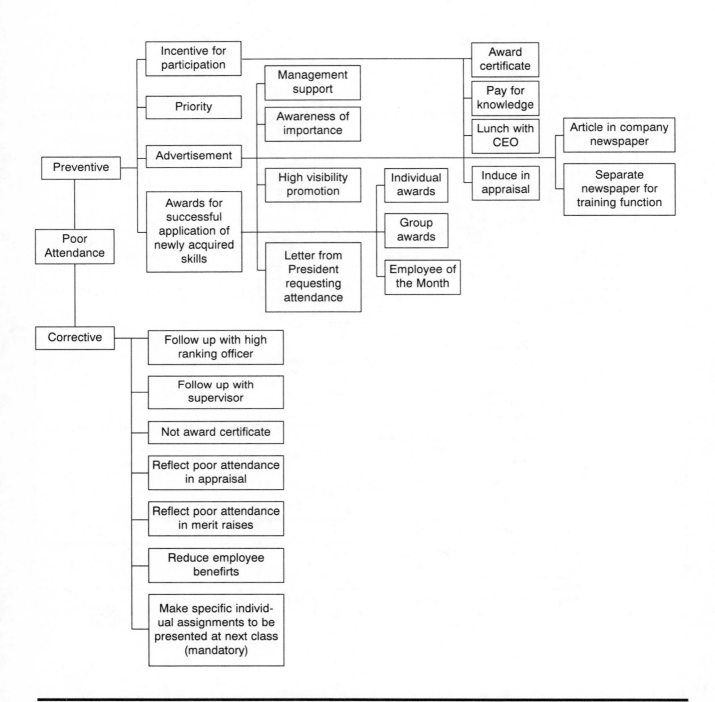

Figure 9-10. This tool systematically maps out in increasing detail the full range of paths and tasks that need to be accomplished in order to achieve a primary goal and every related subgoal. It describes the methods by which every purpose is to be achieved by moving from the abstract to the nitty gritty details of implementation. Used with permission from GOAL/QPC, 13 Branch Street, Methuen, MA 01844-1953. Tel: 508/685-3900.

Source: Brassard M: *The Memory Jogger Plus+: Featuring the Seven Management and Planning Tools, Pocket Cards,* pp 73, 78. © 1989 GOAL/QPC.

FIGURE 9-11
TIMELINE: DRUG-USAGE EVALUATION

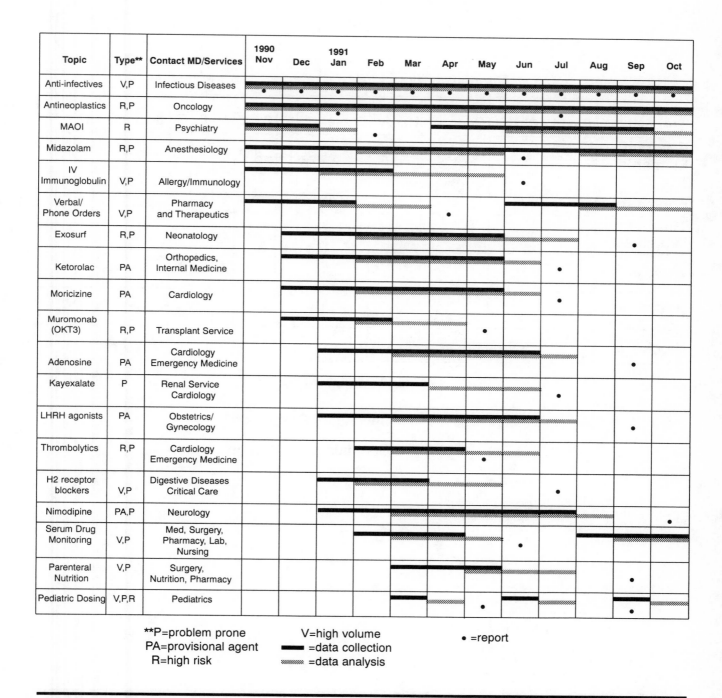

Figure 9-11. This timeline is useful since multiple, concurrent drug-usage evaluation activities may be at different stages and involve different personnel. This chart facilitates the detection and correction of an overly ambitious master plan. Including the contact responsible for collecting data on each topic allows dates for initiation of data collection, data analysis, and reporting to be more realistically established.

Source: Carasiti ME, et al: Integration of drug-usage evaluation with a quality assurance program. *Topics in Hospital Pharmacy Management* 11(2): 13, 1991. Used with permission of Aspen Publishers, Inc.

FIGURE 9-12
TARGET/MEANS MATRIX FOR TARGET

Means (Activity)	Responsibility					Timeline											
	David	Chris	George	Henry	Steve	1	2	3	4	5	6	7	8	9	10	11	12
Program Elements	△	△	△	⊙	△	▲————————▼ (1→4)											
Volume Forecasts	⊙	△	△	△	○	▲————▼ (2→5)											
Throughput Measures	⊙		△	△	○	▲————▼ (5→7)											
Workstations	△		⊙	△	○	▲————▼ (5→7)											
DSGF	△	△	⊙	△	○	▲————▼ (7→9)											
Block	△		○	△	⊙	▲————————▼ (10→12)											

⊙ = Primary Responsibility

○ = Secondary Responsibility

△ = Communication/Needs to Know

Figure 9-12. This tool is used to plan how assigned objectives can be achieved. Action steps are listed down the left side; individuals responsible are across the top. Symbols indicate primary and secondary responsibility for each action and which individuals need to know the specifics of an action. A timeline for each step is also included.

Source: Demers DM: Tutorial: Implementing hoshin planning at the Vermont Academic Medical Center. *Quality Management in Health Care* 1(4): 70, 1993. Used with permission of Aspen Publishers, Inc.

TOOLS FOR KEEPING TEAMS ON TRACK AND KEEPING TRACK OF TEAMS

This section contains a variety of tools to document team activities and to guide teams through the steps necessary to measure, assess, and improve processes. Although teamwork is fundamental to performance improvement, not all the tools in this section apply specifically to the key steps in the Joint Commission's cycle for improving performance.

SECTION TEN

FIGURE 10-1
REQUEST TO START A QUALITY IMPROVEMENT TEAM (QIT)

Directions: If you are interested in starting a QIT, please send the completed form to:

Date submitted:

Name: _____ Work Phone: _____
Job Title: _____
Department/area: _____
Address–Bldg.: _____ Room: _____ Box: _____
Supervisor: _____ Work Phone: _____

1. Briefly describe the current problem or opportunity for improvement:
_____
_____

2. How does the problem impact any of the following areas?

a) the quality of a product or service: _____
_____
_____

b) customer satisfaction: _____
_____
_____

c) working environment:_____
_____
_____

d) cost effectiveness: _____
_____
_____

e) other: _____
_____
_____

Figure 10-1. Staff can use this form to request a charter for a quality improvement team.

Source: Creps LB, et al: Performance improvement review: Implementation of total quality in medical information services. *Topics in Health Information Management* 14(2): 65, 1993. Used with permission of Aspen Publishers, Inc.

FIGURE 10-2
TEAM HISTORY SHEET

Low Back Pain (LBP) Team

Date	Plan	Data/Info Obtained	Conclusion	Next Steps
9/10/93	A. Discuss and decide algorithm boundaries	Group Input: Brainstorming	Algorithm begins: • All patients with back pain present to an MD Algorithm ends: • Resolution of back pain and/or adaptation to limitations in functional level	
	B. Discuss purpose of algorithm		• Decrease cost • Increase quality • Reduce variation; provide a template for working and treatment	
	C. Begin initial encounter portion of algorithm	Emergent conditions needing immediate rule out or treatment: • cauda equina • history of trauma • incapacitating pain • hemo-dynamic instability • history of CA • degree of severity • fever • compression fracture • psychiatric problems • neurologic deficit • substance abuse • first episode or recurrent • infection	 (LBP) ↓ [H&P] ↓ ◇ Acute ◇ acute=LBP for 3 mos or less Team to decide which emergent conditions to include in algorithm	1. Decide which categories of patients to exclude from the algorithm (or write sub-algorithm) 2. Determine a standard initial evaluation, including lab and radiologic tests
		Members Present: Members Absent:	Meeting Evaluation: • Good to define boundaries and purpose • Hard to do • Discussion important • Bogged down with details • May need longer meetings	Next Meeting: October 8, 1993 7:30 AM–9:00 AM 418 South Next Meeting Agenda:

H & P = medical history and physical examination

Figure 10-2. This form can be used by teams in lieu of minutes. The team history sheet reflects the process of the meeting: discussion, conclusions, and assignments. Each completed sheet is a snapshot of a meeting; sheets are easy to review and can be used to track meetings across time as issues are raised, resolved, or acted on.

Source: Lutheran General HealthSystem, Park Ridge, IL, 1993. Used with permission.

FIGURE 10-3 (A)
PROJECT GRIDS: CHARTERED TEAMS

Project Name	Leader/Facilitator/Mentor	Description	Aim	Boundaries	Key Quality Characteristic(s)	Start Date (SD)/Estimated Time of Completion (ETC)	Comments
Acute Chest Pain Management	L: Cooks, MD F: Ryan/Corry	Process of medical evaluation and management of patients presenting to the ER w/complaint of chest pain	•Rapidly identify patients with cardiac-related chest pain •Implement appropriate medical management	Begins: Notification of pt arrival or intent to arrive at ER Ends: with definitive medical diagnosis and initiation of treatment plan		SD: 8/93 ETC: > 1 year	•Algorithm being developed •ER process being developed
Blood Transfusion	L: Okumo, MD F: Schmidt M: Shaffer, MD	Process by which blood transfusion ordered by physicians are given to a pt at LGAS	To have a process in place which insures the right blood is given to the right patient	Begins: Patient identified Ends: Patient receives blood	Accurate blood product	SD: 5/92 ETC: > 1 year	
Clinical Billing Systems Design	L: Gregor F: Ryan, PhD	Process through which clinical record originates charges that drive billing system	Improve the clinical documentation system and its linkage to the charge system to successfully drive the billing system	Begins: Assessment of capacity of medical record to capture charges Ends: Redesign of medical record		SD: 3/93 ETC: 3/94	
Clinical Management of Oral Anticoagulation Therapy Center	L: Sacks, MD F. Brugher	Process of educating patients re: the use of Coumadin, monitoring the level of anticoagulation, and prescribing Coumadin to maintain appropriate level of anticoagulation	Improve patient outcomes by monitoring, evaluating, educating, diagnosing, and prescribing for outpatients to maintain appropriate level of oral anticoagulation utilizing the guidelines and algorithm for Coumadin management development by LGHP and simultaneously evaluate the efficacy of the algorithm and modify as necessary to optimize outcomes	Begins: Upon referral of pt to outpatient anticoagulation therapy program for Coumadin management Ends: Upon completion of Coumadin therapy or if pt falls outside the boundaries of the management algorithm due to complications, recurrent disease, or concurrent medical problems	% of patients with complications, major/minor bleeding, symptom recurrence requiring clinical intervention		•Center operating •Data being collected •Research design being developed
Continuous Care D/C Instructions	L: F:	A portion of D/C process for continuous care of pt specifically; D/C instructions sent to the next provider	Design a process to meet Joint Commission requirement for above	Begins: When discharge order is given Ends: When patient receives information to give to next provider			Assigned to line

Figure 10-3. The project grids in this figure can be used to track improvement initiatives in progress. The grid, 10-3(A), describes the project, its boundaries, its purpose, key quality characteristics, and start/end time. The report, 10-3(B), provides a quick overview of the organization's quality efforts for purposes of planning and monitoring of resource use.

Source: Lutheran General HealthSystem, Park Ridge, IL, 1993. Used with permission.

FIGURE 10-3 (B)
PROJECT GRIDS: CHARTERED TEAMS

Name of Project	Major Accomplishments	Major Remaining Tasks
Acute Chest Pain Management	N/A (The team was chartered at July 1993 meeting)	Workplan: •Organize a team •Define patient populations of interest •Prioritize opportunities for process improvements •Initiate process improvement
Bed Assignment	•Recovery room calls to admitting decreased •Earlier committee recommendations revisited •Group is developing more trust and focus	Team to focus on 3 areas: •Implementation of prior issues raised by Admitting Team •Measurements of process to be developed and tracked •Expansion to PMs for clinical/clerical team to be planned/addressed
Blood Transfusion	•Currently in "C" phase of focus •Developing detailed flowchart	•Operational define KQC (patient receives correct blood) •Collect data on KQC Select strategy for improvement
Clinical Billing	•Identified causes of error in current charge system •Determined LGHS can produce accurate bill from clinical record, but existing medical records need to be revised •Flowcharted processes through which written medical record and electronic medical record are designed/revised •Determined KQC: number of patient complaints about errors in charging. Collected baseline data re: KQC and determined process is not in control •Inventoried total set of medical records used for charging •Inventoried all sources of charging not on medical records	•Redesign inpatient medical record to capture charges •Integrate outpatient with inpatient records
Clinical Management of Oral Anticoagulation Therapy	•Algorithm developed/implemented at LGHP •Clinic ready for start-up	•Development of research design •Data collection (1 year) •Data analysis

KQC=key quality characteristic

FIGURE 10-4
A PLAN-DO-CHECK-ACT WORKSHEET

1. What are we trying to accomplish?

Some questions to consider: (a) What is our aim? (b) What need is tied to that aim? What exactly do we know about that need? (c) What is the process we are working on? (d) What is the link between our aim and this process? Does this process offer us the most leverage for work in support of our aim? (e) What background information do we have available about this improvement—customer, other?

2. How will we know that a change is an improvement?

Some questions to consider: (a) Who are the customers? What would constitute improvement in their eyes? (b) What is the output of the process? (c) How does the process work? (d) How does the process currently vary?

3. What changes *can* we make that we predict will lead to improvement?

Some questions to consider: (a) Reflecting on the process described, are there ideas for improvement that come readily to mind? (b) Would a simple decision matrix help you decide which to work on first? (c) Are all our decision criteria worded to make their scoring in the same direction? (d) For the change we'd like to try, what is our prediction? (e) What questions do we have about the change, the process, and our prediction? What will you need to check? Do these questions help us link to the overall aim and need?

4. How shall we PLAN the pilot?

Some questions to consider: (a) Who is going to do What, by When, Where, and How? (b) Is the "owner" of the process involved? (c) How shall we measure to answer our questions—to confirm or reject our prediction?

Figure 10-4. This worksheet can help teams or workgroups as they move through the plan-do-check-act improvement process. The worksheet poses key questions to be answered.

Source: Batalden PB, Stoltz PK: A framework for the continual improvement of health care: Building and applying professional and improvement knowledge to test changes in daily work. *The Joint Commission Journal on Quality Improvement* 19(10): 446–447, 1993. Worksheet developed with the help of Tom Nolan, PhD, of Associates in Process Improvement. ©1992 HCA Quality Resource Group, Jun 1993. Permission to dulplicate granted if source cited.

FIGURE 10-4 (CONTINUED)
A PLAN-DO-CHECK-ACT WORKSHEET

5. What are we learning as we DO the pilot?

Some questions to consider: (a) What have we learned from our planned pilot and collection of information? (b) What have we learned from the unplanned information we collected? (c) Was the pilot congruent with the plan?

6. As we CHECK and study what happened, what have we learned?

Some questions to consider: (a) Was our prediction correct? (b) Did the pilot work better for all types of customers—or just some of them? (c) What did we learn about planning the next change?

7. As we ACT to hold the gains or abandon our pilot efforts, what needs to be done?

Some questions to consider: (a) What should be standardized? (b) What training should be considered to provide continuity? (c) How should continued monitoring be undertaken? (d) If the pilot efforts should be abandoned, what has been learned?

8. Looking back over the whole pilot, what have we learned?

Some questions to consider: (a) What was learned that we expected to learn? (b) What unanticipated things did we learn? (c) What did we learn about our predictive ability? (d) Who might be interested in learning what we've learned?

FIGURE 10-5
PROJECT CHECKLIST FOR TEAMS

	YES	NO
Have you flowcharted the process?	❏	❏
Is this something within your team's span of control?	❏	❏
Do you have a member from each part of the process?	❏	❏
Have you checked to see if other teams are working on something similar?	❏	❏
Have you developed ground rules that everyone agrees to?	❏	❏
Have you selected a team leader and team facilitator?	❏	❏
Do all team members understand their roles?	❏	❏
Have you done a commitment analysis?	❏	❏
Do you know where to go to get help?	❏	❏
Will everyone be able to see the results?	❏	❏
What will the project cost?	❏	❏
What will it save?	❏	❏

Figure 10-5. This checklist is designed to help improvement teams ensure they can effectively address the process they plan to tackle.

Source: © 1993 Organizational Learning Group, Mount Pleasant, South Carolina.

FIGURE 10-6
PROGRESS CHECKLIST

Instructions: Refer to this list occasionally to monitor the team's progress. This list can also give you clues of what to do if your team gets stuck between phases of the project. Some of these items may not pertain to your team—or you may be able to identify other milestones that are not listed here that you want to add.

Mission Statement
__Receive from management
__Clarify; modify if necessary
__Get management approval for mission revisions
__Define goals and objectives related to mission

Planning
__Select team members
__Develop logistical system for team meetings
__Create improvement plan
__Develop a top-down flowchart of project stages

Education/Team-Building Activities
__Introduce team members
__Explain roles and expectations
__Orient to group's process
__Introduce basics of new approach: 14 points, Joiner triangle, key quality improvement concepts
__Provide training in needed scientific tools
__Develop ownership in project

Study the Process
__Construct top-down flowchart of process
__Interview customers to identify needs
__Design data-gathering procedures
__Gather data on process
__Analyze data to see if process is stable
__Identify problems with process

Localize Problems
__Identify possible causes of problems
__Select likely causes
__Gather data to establish root causes
__Analyze data
__Rank causes
__Develop appropriate, permanent solutions

Make Changes/Document Improvement
__Develop a strategic plan to test changes
__Implement test
__Gather data on new process
__Analyze data on new process
__Analyze data, critique changes in light of data
__Redesign improvements in process and repeat this step if necessary
__Implement further changes, or refer matter to appropriate person or group
__Monitor results of changes
__Establish a system to monitor in the future

Closure
__Prepare presentation on project
__Deliver presentation
__Evaluate team's progress
__Evaluate team's product
__Document

Figure 10-6. This list can be used to oversee a group's progress. It can also give clues about what to do if progress is stalled.

Source: Scholtes PR: *The Team Handbook*. Madison, WI: Joiner Associates, Inc, 1988, p 40. All rights reserved. Used with permission.

FIGURE 10-7
BASIC STORYBOARD FORMAT

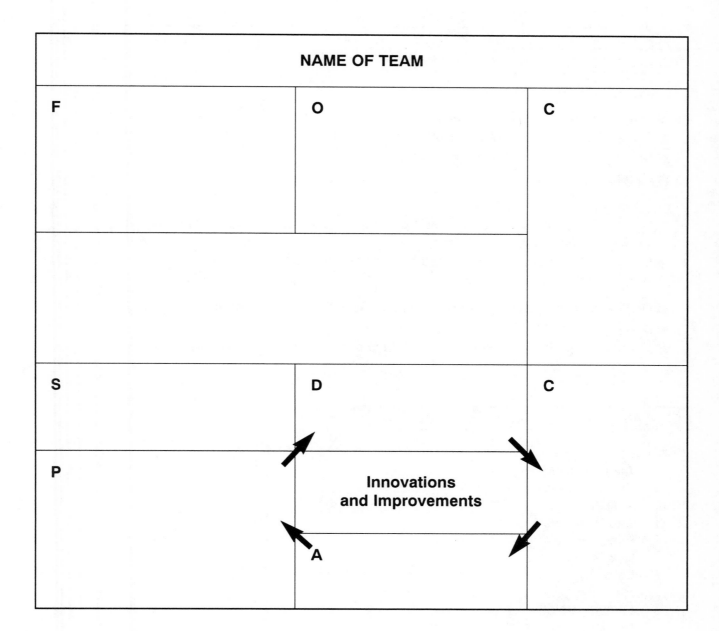

Figure 10-7. This is one format for constructing a storyboard to display a team's activities and improvements. This format follows the FOCUS-PDCA process. Team activities for each step are documented using written descriptions, charts, and graphs, as appropriate. Storyboards are often posted in the facility so others can see the team's activity. They are also useful for keeping teams on track. Figures 10-8 and 10-9 are examples of completed storyboards (using somewhat different formats than this figure).

Source: West Paces Medical Center, Atlanta, GA, 1993. Used with permission.

FIGURE 10-8
STORYBOARD FORMAT

Facility: Lutheran General Hospital HealthSystem	Contact:
Project: Laboratory CSF Processing	Phone:

Find a process to improve

Origin
- Insufficient quantity of speciman
- Turnaround time (TAT) was too long
- No single location for specimen storage
- Orders not clarified

Boundaries
- Begins: The point at which the CSF specimen is received in the specimen-receiving area of the laboratory
- Ends: The point at which the laboratory reports the results

Aim
- Decrease number of CSF specimens received with insufficient quantity
- Decrease TAT of CSF processing
- Decrease time to locate sufficient volume of specimen to perform ordered tests

Organize an effort to work on improvement

- Team Leader:
  - Takashi Okuno, MD,
    Clinical Laboratories
- Facilitator
- Team Members:
  - Bacteriology
  - Biochemistry
  - Cytology
  - Hematology
  - Immunovirology
  - Laboratory Administration
  - Laboratory Quality Assurance
  - Laboratory Info Specimen Acquisition

Figure 10-8. This example of a storyboard format uses the FOCUS improvement process and includes team members, flowcharts, key quality characteristics, and results. Storyboards such as this one can be used to gather information and to make formal and informal presentations. This type of storyboard provides an overview of the process the team followed in its efforts.

Source: Lutheran General HealthSystem, Park Ridge, IL. Used with permission.

FIGURE 10-8 (CONTINUED)
STORYBOARD FORMAT

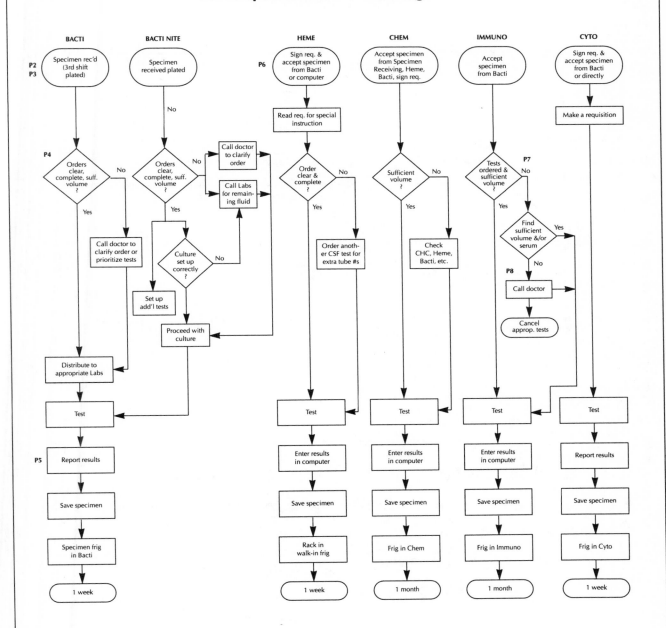

Clarify current knowledge of the process

CSF Departmental Processing

Key Quality Characteristics: Accurate and timely results of CSF specimens

■ Percent of CSF specimens received with any of the following problems:
- Insufficient specimen
- Mislabeled specimen
- Lost specimen
- Unclear specimen
- Other

■ Number of telephone calls that Bacteriology must make because of problems with CSF specimens
■ Departmental satisfaction with CSF process

FIGURE 10-8 (CONTINUED)
STORYBOARD FORMAT

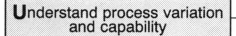

Understand process variation and capability

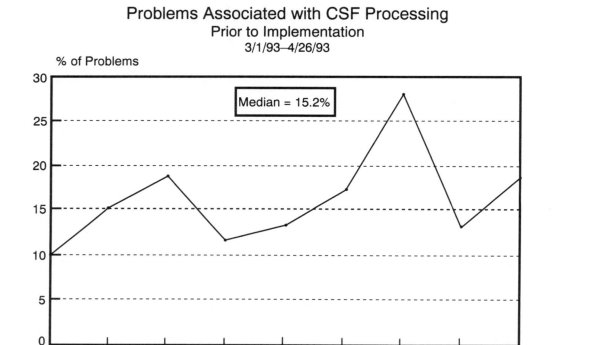

Problems Associated with CSF Processing
Prior to Implementation
3/1/93–4/26/93

% of Problems

Median = 15.2%

* Percent of problems calculated: $\frac{\text{total of problems}}{\text{\# of samples}}$

Lessons Learned

- ■ Important for each laboratory section to understand each other's process
- ■ Boundaries need to be workable and within the scope of authority of the group
- ■ Imperative to simplify the process and reduce variation
- ■ Very difficult to stay within the meeting time allotted
- ■ The CQI process is a lot of work!
- ■ Intense staff level involvement would be much more difficult
- ■ Meeting minutes, Flowcharts, and Data Collection required a lot of preparation time
- ■ Data collection continues after implementation of the process improvement

FIGURE 10-8 (CONTINUED)
STORYBOARD FORMAT

Select a strategy for continued improvement

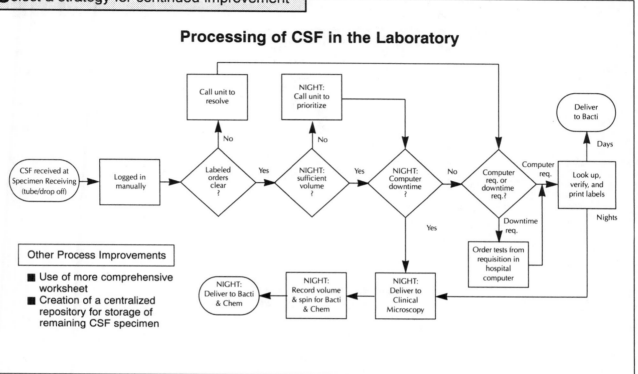

Processing of CSF in the Laboratory

Other Process Improvements

- Use of more comprehensive worksheet
- Creation of a centralized repository for storage of remaining CSF specimen

Major Accomplishments

- Modified the CSF HIS computer screen
- Educated medical staff about testing requirements
- Communicated time Bacteriology ends processing at night
- Communicated the cut-off time between third and first shift
- Modified the CSF worksheet to obtain all the necessary signatures and centralize information for the data-collection process
- Created a centrally located CSF retention location
- Modified reporting on the computer-generated patient summary. Now all CSF results are consolidated into one location.

Problems Associated with CSF Processing
3/1/93–8/23/93

% of Problems

Prior to Implementation

After Implementation

Median = 15.2%

Median = 5.4%

30

25

20

15

10

5

0

3/1 3/8 3/15 3/22 3/29 4/5 4/12 4/19 4/26 5/3 5/10 5/17 5/24 5/31 6/7 6/14 6/21 6/28 7/5 7/12 7/19 7/26 8/2 8/9 8/16 8/23

*Percent of problems calculated: $\dfrac{\text{total of problems}}{\text{\# of samples}}$

FIGURE 10-9
PICTURE BOOK FORMAT

This Picture Book Format was adapted from a classic quality improvement anecdote published in the booklet "The Quest for Higher Quality: The Deming Prize and Quality Control" published by RICOH of America, Inc.

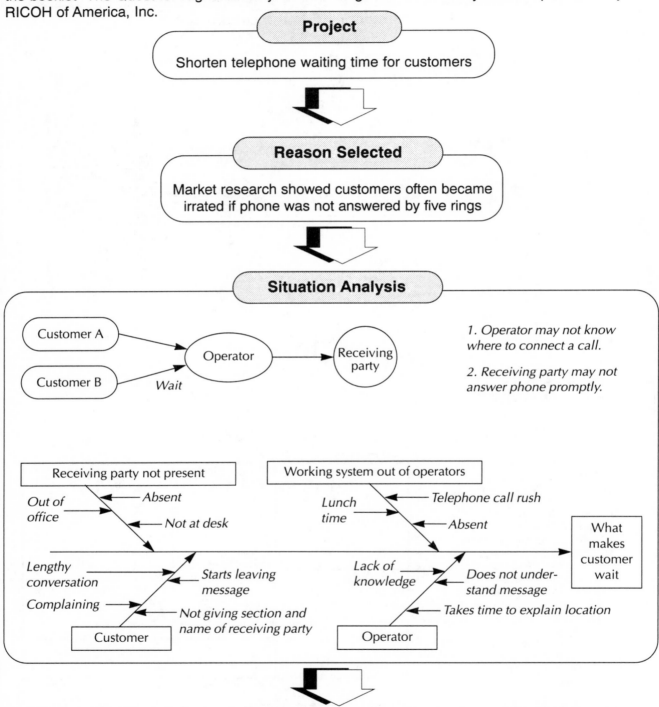

Figure 10-9. These pages show in detail one type of picture book format. This format uses words, charts, and graphs to illustrate the following information on an improvement effort: project, reason selected, situation analysis, data collection, data analysis, Pareto diagram (causal analysis), goal, actions, and evaluation.

FIGURE 10-9 (CONTINUED)
PICTURE BOOK FORMAT

Data Collection

Check Sheet

Date \ Reason	No one present in the section receiving the call	Receiving party not present	Only one operator		Total
June 4	\\\\\	⫴⫴ \	⫴⫴ ⫴⫴ \		24
June 5	⫴⫴	⫴⫴ ⫴⫴	⫴⫴ ⫴⫴ ⫴⫴⫴		32
June 6	⫴⫴ \	⫴⫴	⫴⫴ ⫴⫴ ⫴⫴		28
⋮					
June 15	⫴⫴	⫴⫴	⫴⫴ ⫴⫴⫴		25

Data Analysis

Reasons why callers had to wait

		Daily average	Total number
A	One operator (partner out of the office)	14.3	172
B	Receiving party not present	6.1	73
C	No one present in the section receiving the call	5.1	61
D	Section and name of receiving party not given	1.6	19
E	Inquiry about branch office locations	1.3	16
F	Other reasons	0.8	10
	Total	29.2*	351

* 6% of calls had long waits

FIGURE 10-9 (CONTINUED)
PICTURE BOOK FORMAT

Pareto Diagram

A	One operator (partner out of the office)
B	Receiving party not present
C	No one present in the section receiving the call
D	Section and name of receiving party not given
E	Inquiry about branch office locations
F	Other reasons

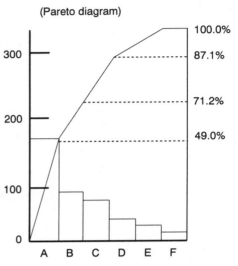

(Pareto diagram)

Goal

Reduce calls with long waits to zero

Actions

1. Helper operator brought in from clerical section to substitute while each of the two regular operators went to lunch.

2. Asked all employees to leave messages when leaving their desks.

3. Compiled directory listing personnel and their respective jobs.

FIGURE 10-9 (CONTINUED)
PICTURE BOOK FORMAT

Evaluation

Comparison of before and after

	Reasons why callers had to wait	Total number Before	Total number After	Daily average Before	Daily average After
A	One operator (partner out of the office)	172	15	14.3	1.2
B	Receiving party not present	73	17	6.1	1.4
C	No one present in the section receiving the call	61	20	5.1	1.7
D	Section and name of receiving party not given	19	4	1.6	0.3
E	Inquiry about branch office locations	16	3	1.3	0.2
F	Other reasons	10	0	0.8	0
		351	59	29.2*	4.8

Period: 12 days from Aug. 17 to 30

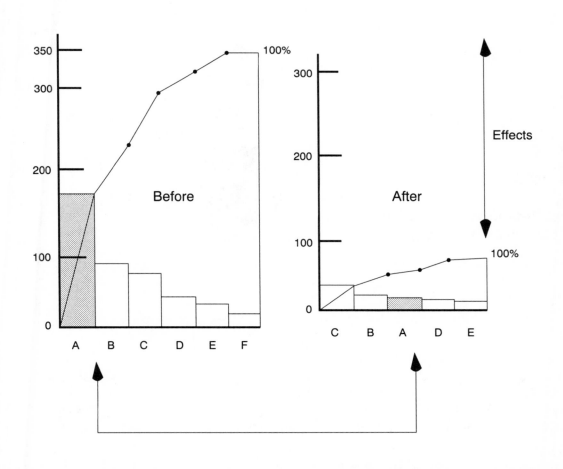

FIGURE 10-10
WALL OF FAME DISPLAY

Community Medical Center
Process Improvement Team Information

Maximizing Surgical Utilization Team

Holding the Gains
Check performance
Monitor control system

Remedial Journey
Consider alternative solution
Design solutions and controls
Address resistance to change
Implement solutions and control

Diagnostic Journey
Analyze symptoms
Formulate theories of causes
Test theories
Identify root causes

**Project Definition
and Organization**
Define project and team

First Meeting Date: May 24, 1991

Team Members:

**Project Definition: Revise process for
each surgical service point.**

Figure 10-10. This format communicates improvement activities while they are underway and increases employee recognition. The "Wall of Fame" display tracks a team's progress on a graphic of a thermometer. The terms "diagnostic journey" and "remedial journey" used to define the project's stages were originally coined by Joseph Juran.

Source: Keeping recognition programs 'fresh' requires innovation. QI/TQM, Jul 1993, p 97. Used with permission of Total Quality Management, Community Medical Center, Toms River, NJ. Cherise Kaplan, Designer.

FIGURE 10-11
HALL OF FAME DISPLAY

Pharmacy IV Waste Team

January 1993
Team Duration: 14 Months

Start Date: 11/91

Project Definition

Decrease IV Waste
in Department

Lender   Facilitator

Changes/Enhancements to the IV Process Hospitalwide

• Initially, IV was made 24 hours in advance, delivered, and picked up next day patient was discharged

• After the process was changed/enhanced, IV was now made 4 to 8 hours before due and delivered in 1–2 hours

• The above enhancements as of January 1993 still in place

Monitoring Information

• The weekly amount of $1,200 for IV was reduced to $200 due to process

• The process and cost savings have been monitored for 2 years to date

• The pharmacy staff is responsible for monitoring the gains

• The IV process is monitored on a weekly basis using graphs

What is the Measure of Success?

• The measure of success for the IV waste process is maintaining the gains and cost savings of $1,000 weekly.

• Within the monitoring process, the team strives to maintain and ensure efficiency and cost savings by making corrections when necessary.

Color photo of team is put here for display

Figure 10-11. This figure shows how an organization can communicate results of improvement efforts and increase employee recognition. The "Hall of Fame" display includes the improvement team's original project definition, its accomplishments, any changes it has effected, the subjects that the team continues to monitor, and a color photograph of the team.

Source: Keeping recognition programs 'fresh' requires innovation. QI/TQM, Jul 1993, p 96. Used with permission of Total Quality Management, Community Medical Center, Toms River, NJ. Cherise Kaplan, Designer.

FIGURE 10-12
TEAM MEETING DOCUMENTATION

Team _____ **Date** _____

Members Present [Note roles—(L)eader, (R)ecorder, (T)imekeeper, (F)acilitator]:

_____

_____

Step: F O C U S P D C A (Circle one and give activity under "Proceedings")

Proceedings (See below for details on methods/steps) _____

_____

_____

_____

_____

_____

_____

Next Agenda: _____

_____

_____

Evaluation:
Did Well: _____

_____

Could Do Better: _____

_____

Helpful Hints for Each Step

Find a process to improve: Opportunity statement with beginning and ending boundaries and customers specified; why is it important to improve this process now?

Organize a team that knows the process: List team members with title, department, position; are employees who are closest to the process on the team?

Clarify current knowledge of the process: Flowchart the process; show other clarification of current process; obvious improvement (low-hanging fruit), if any.

Understand sources of process variation: Cause and effect diagram: define key quality characteristics; description/display of initial data collection; obvious improvements (low-hanging fruit), if any.

Select the process improvement: List and prioritize ideas for improvement; which is the best one to work on first?

Plan the improvement: Description of plan for action—who, what, where, when, how.

Do the improvement: Dates of implementation; description of any variation from plan.

Check the results: Data collection and display; lessons learned.

Act to hold the gain: Comparison to initial data; assessment/conclusions; action plan.

Figure 10-12. This two-page format helps teams ensure that their meetings address the steps in the FOCUS-PDCA process. The format includes space to briefly plan the next meeting and to evaluate the meeting just completed.

10-13

10-14

FIGURE 10-13
MEETING AGENDA

	Time	Person Responsible
Team _____ Leader _____		
Date _____ Recorder _____		
Time _____ Timekeeper _____		
Place _____ Facilitator _____		

	Time	Person Responsible
1. Clarify Objective: _____ _____		
2. Review Roles	_____	_____
3. Review Agenda (Proposed Format)		
4. Work Through Agenda Items A. _____	_____	_____
B. _____	_____	_____
C. _____	_____	_____
D. _____	_____	_____
E. _____	_____	_____
5. Review Minutes	_____	_____
6. Evaluate Meeting	_____	_____
7. Plan Next Agenda	_____	_____

Figure 10-13. This sample format helps teams and other groups organize meetings and ensure that tasks have a designated timeframe and responsible party.

FIGURE 10-14
MEETING MINUTES

Team _____   Leader _____

Date _____   Recorder _____

Time _____   Timekeeper _____

Place _____   Facilitator _____

Members Present

_____

_____

_____

1. Clarified Objective _____

2. Reviewed Roles

3. Reviewed Agenda

4. Worked Through Agenda Items

A. _____

_____

B. _____

_____

C. _____

_____

D. _____

_____

5. Reviewed Minutes

6. Evaluated   1   2   3   4   5   6   7   8   9   10 (optional)

           Poor   *Excellent*

Did Well _____

Could Improve _____

7. Planned Next Agenda

Figure 10-14. This format for recording meeting minutes helps ensure that all relevant information is included; the format also includes a self-evaluation of the meeting.